The Hierarchy of Saints

Part 2

The Hierarchy of Saints

Part 2

Spiritual Discourses of Shaykh Muhammad Hisham Kabbani

PUBLISHED BY
INSTITUTE FOR SPIRITUAL AND CULTURAL ADVANCEMENT

Published and Distributed by:

Institute for Spiritual and Cultural Advancement (ISCA)
17195 Silver Parkway, #201
Fenton, MI 48430 USA
Tel: (888) 278-6624
Fax: (810) 815-0518
Email: staff@naqshbandi.org
Web: http://www.naqshbandi.org

First Edition: March 2013
THE HIERARCHY OF SAINTS, PART 2
ISBN: 978-1-938058-03-5

Library of Congress Cataloging-in-Publication Data

Kabbani, Muhammad Hisham.
Spiritual discourses of Shaykh Muhammad Hisham Kabbani. -- 1st ed.
p. cm. -- (The hierarchy of saints, part 2)
Includes bibliographical references.
ISBN 978-1-938058-03-5 (alk. paper)
1. Naqshabandiyah. 2. Sufism. I. Title.
BP189.7.N352K327 2010
297.4'8--dc22
2010044186

PRINTED IN THE UNITED STATES OF AMERICA
15 14 13 12 11 05 06 07 08 09

Mawlana Shaykh Hisham Kabbani inaugurates *Ramadan Series 2010* in the renowned Naqshbandi *zawiya* in Michigan, where, since 1999, he continues the Ramadan tradition of reciting the *awrad* in congregation before sunrise, accompanied by an inspired spiritual discourse. The popular Ramadan program has been broadcast live on Sufilive.com since 2005 and reaches ten of thousands of viewers worldwide. (August 2010)

Table of Contents

About the Author

World-renowned religious scholar, Shaykh Muhammad Hisham Kabbani is featured in the ground-breaking book published by Georgetown University, *The 500 Most Influential Muslims in the World*. For decades he has promoted traditional Islamic principles of peace, tolerance, love, compassion and brotherhood, while rigorously opposing extremism in all its forms. He hails from a respected family of traditional Islamic scholars, which includes the former head of the Association of Muslim Scholars of Lebanon and the present grand mufti (highest Islamic religious authority) of Lebanon.

Shaykh Kabbani is highly trained, both as a western scientist and an Islamic scholar. He received a bachelor's degree in chemistry and later studied medicine. Under the instruction of Shaykh ʿAbdAllāh ad-Daghestani, upon whose personal notes this book is based, he holds a degree in Islamic Divine Law. Shaykh Muḥammad Nazim Adil al-Haqqani, world leader of the Naqshbandi-Haqqani Sufi Order, authorized him to teach and counsel students in Sufism.

In his long-standing endeavor to promote a better understanding of traditional Islam, in February 2010, Shaykh Kabbani hosted HRH Charles, the Prince of Wales at a cultural event at the revered Old Trafford Stadium in Manchester, U.K. He has hosted two international conferences in the U.S., and regional conferences on a host of issues, which attracted moderate Muslim scholars from Asia, the Far East, Middle East, Africa, U.K. and Eastern Europe. His counsel is sought by journalists, academics, policymakers and government leaders.

For thirty years, Shaykh Kabbani has consistently promoted peaceful cooperation among people of all beliefs. Since the early 1990s, he has launched numerous endeavors to bring moderate Muslims into the mainstream. Often at great personal risk, he has been instrumental in awakening Muslim social consciousness regarding the religious duty to stand firm against extremism and terrorism, for the benefit of all. His bright, hopeful outlook, with a goal to honor and serve all humanity, has helped millions understand the difference between moderate mainstream Muslims and minority extremist sects.

In the United States, Shaykh Kabbani serves as Chairman, Islamic Supreme Council of America; Founder, Naqshbandi Sufi Order of America; Advisor, World Organization for Resource Development and Education; Chairman, As-Sunnah Foundation of America; Founder, *The Muslim Magazine*. In the United Kingdom, Shaykh Kabbani is an advisor to Sufi Muslim Council, which consults to the British government on public policy and social and religious issues.

Other titles by Shaykh Kabbani include: *At the Feet of My Master* (2010, 2 vols.), *The Nine-fold Ascent* (2009), *Banquet for the Soul* (2008), *Illuminations* (2007), *Universe Rising* (2007), *Symphony of Remembrance* (2007), *A Spiritual Commentary on the Chapter of Sincerity* (2006), *The Sufi Science of Self-Realization* (Fons Vitae, 2005), *Keys to the Divine Kingdom* (2005), *Classical Islam and the Naqshbandi Sufi Order* (2004), *The Naqshbandi Sufi Tradition Guidebook* (2004), *The Approach of Armageddon? An Islamic Perspective* (2003), *Encyclopedia of Muḥammad's Women Companions and the Traditions They Related* (1998, with Dr. Laleh Bakhtiar), *Encyclopedia of Islamic Doctrine* (7 vols. 1998), *Angels Unveiled* (1996), *The Naqshbandi Sufi Way* (1995), *and Remembrance of God Liturgy of the Sufi Naqshbandi Masters* (1994).

Preface

This book is based on the divinely inspired spiritual discourses of the global head of the Naqshbandi-Haqqani Sufi Order, Mawlana Shaykh Nazim Adil al-Haqqani, and his representative, Mawlana Shaykh Hisham Kabbani. It is a compilation of Shaykh Kabbani's *ṣuḥbah* from the annual "Ramadan Series" (2010), which is devoted to ancient sacred teachings of forty generations of eminent Sufi masters of the Naqshbandi Golden Chain.

The Hierarchy of Saints, Part 2 reveals rare, secret knowledge that is only assimilated by adhering to the protocols of the highest Sufi masters. It takes us on a journey that, through discipline and steadfastness, subjugates the ego and worldly desires and reveals one's unique path to receive "the Sacred Trust".

This volume outlines advanced levels of conduct and character that, under supervision of the Sufi master, bring one into higher spiritual realms. The stations of *Ikhlas* (Sincerity) and *Tawhid* (Oneness) are highlighted, along with the disciplines to reach them and many traps to avoid. Descriptions of the premier shaykhs that look after affairs of this world are both insightful and captivating. Lessons of previous masters and their students offer the seeker a road map to success.

This title is recommended for anyone engaged in the study Sufism.

Publisher's Notes

This book is directed to those familiar with the Sufi Way; however, to accommodate lay readers unfamiliar with Sufi terminology and practices, we have provided English translations of Arabic texts and a comprehensive glossary. Where Arabic terms are crucial to the discussion, we have included transliteration and footnoted explanations. For readers familiar with Arabic and Islamic teachings, for further clarity please consult the cited sources.

The original material is based on transcripts of a series of holy gatherings which serve as conduits of heavenly guidance. The *ṣuḥbah,* a divinely inspired talk which conveys powerful energy that uplifts the soul, is delivered by the "shaykh," a highly trained spiritual guide. To present the authentic flavor of such rare teachings, great care was taken to preserve the speaking styles of both the author and the illustrious shaykhs upon whose notes this book is based. Please pray that our shortcomings are corrected.

Translations from Arabic to English pose unique challenges which we have tried our best to make understandable to Western readers. In addition, please note the worldwide cultural practice of not including the definite article "the," as in "~~the~~ Prophet," which is a more intimate reference that appears occasionally throughout this work.

Quotes from the Holy Qur'an are offset with chapter and verse cited. The Holy Traditions of Prophet Muḥammad (*āḥadīth)* are offset and cited, in most cases. Historic dates are often referenced as "Hijri" and "A.H." (After Hijri), which is the commencement of the Islamic calendar, when Prophet Muḥammad migrated from Mecca to Madinah in 622 C.E. (Christian Era) to escape religious persecution and form his early nation. A reference calendar has also been provided.

Where gender-specific pronouns such as "he" and "him" are applied in a general sense, no discrimination is intended towards women, upon whom The Almighty bestowed great honor.

Islamic teachings are primarily based on four sources, in this order:

- **Holy Qur'an**: the holy book of divine revelation (God's Word) granted to Prophet Muḥammad. Reference to Holy Qur'an appears as "4:12," indicating "Chapter 4, Verse 12."
- **Sunnah**: holy traditions of Prophet Muḥammad ﷺ; the systematic recording of his words and actions that comprise the *ḥadīth*. For fifteen

centuries, Islam has applied a strict, highly technical standard, rating each narration in terms of its authenticity and categorizing its "transmission." As this book is not highly technical, we simplified the reporting of *ḥadīth*, but included the narrator and source texts to support the discussion at hand.

- ***Ijma'***: The adherence, or agreement of the experts of independent reasoning *(āhl al-ijtihād)* to the conclusions of a given ruling pertaining to what is permitted and what is forbidden after the passing of the Prophet, Peace be upon him, as well as the agreement of the Community of Muslims concerning what is obligatorily known of the religion with its decisive proofs. Perhaps a clearer statement of this principle is, "We do not separate (in belief and practice) from the largest group of the Muslims."
- **Legal Rulings:** highly trained Islamic scholars form legal rulings from their interpretation of the Qur'an and the Sunnah, known as *ijtihād*. Such rulings are intended to provide Muslims an Islamic context regarding contemporary social norms. In theological terms, scholars who form legal opinions have completed many years of rigorous training and possess degrees similar to a doctorate in divinity in Islamic knowledge, or in legal terms, hold the status of a high court or supreme court judge, or higher.

The following universally recognized symbols have been respectfully included in this work. While they may seem tedious, they are deeply appreciated by a vast majority of our readers.

ﷻ *Subḥānahu wa Ta'alā* (may His Glory be Exalted), recited after the name "Allāh" and any of the Islamic names of God.

ﷺ *ṢallAllāhu 'alayhi wa sallam* (God's blessings and greetings of peace be upon him), recited after the holy name of Prophet Muḥammad.

عليه السلام *'Alayhi 's-salām* (peace be upon him/her), recited after holy names of other prophets, names of Prophet Muḥammad's relatives, the pure and virtuous women in Islam, and angels.

رضي الله عنه / رضي الله عنها *RaḍīAllāhu 'anh(um)* (may God be pleased with him/her), recited after the holy names of Companions of Prophet Muḥammad; plural: *raḍīAllāhu 'anhum.*

ق represents *QaddasAllāhu sirrah* (may God sanctify his secret), recited after names of saints.

Transliteration

Transliteration from Arabic to English poses challenges. To show respect, Muslims often capitalize nouns which, in English, normally appear in lowercase. To facilitate authentic pronunciation of names, places and terms, use the following key:

Symbol	Transliteration	Symbol	Transliteration	Vowels: Long	
ء	’	ط	ṭ	آ ى	ā
ب	b	ظ	ẓ	و	ū
ت	t	ع	‘	ي	ī
ث	th	غ	gh	**Short**	
ج	j	ف	f	َ	a
ح	ḥ	ق	q	ُ	u
خ	kh	ك	k	ِ	i
د	d	ل	l		
ذ	dh	م	m		
ر	r	ن	n		
ز	z	ه	h		
س	s	و	w		
ش	sh	ي	y		
ص	ṣ	ة	ah; at		
ض	ḍ	ال	al-/’l-		

Masters of the Naqshbandi-Haqqani Golden Chain

May Allāh ﷻ preserve their secrets.

1. Prophet Muḥammad ibn ʿAbdAllāh ﷺ
2. Abū Bakr as-Ṣiddīq ق
3. Salmān al-Farsi ق
4. Qasim bin Muḥammad bin Abū Bakr ق
5. Jafar aṣ-Ṣādiq ق
6. Tayfur Abū Yazīd al-Bistāmi ق
7. AbūlHassan ʿAlī al-Kharqani ق
8. Abū ʿAlī al-Farmadi ق
9. Abū Yaqub Yusuf al-Hamadani ق
10. AbūlAbbas, al-Khiḍr ق
11. ʿAbdul Khāliq al-Ghujdawāni ق
12. Arif ar-Riwakri ق
13. Khwaja Maḥmūd al-Anjir al-Faghnawi ق
14. ʿAlī ar-Ramitani ق
15. Muḥammad Baba as-Samasi ق
16. as-Sayyid Amir Kulal ق
17. Muḥammad Bahaʿuddin Shah Naqshband ق
18. Alaʿuddin al-Bukhāri al-Attar ق
19. Yaqub al-Charkhi ق
20. Ubaydullāh al-Ahrar ق
21. Muḥammad az-Zahid ق
22. Darwish Muḥammad ق
23. Muḥammad Khwaja al-Amkanaki ق
24. Muḥammad al-Baqi billāh ق
25. Aḥmad al-Farūqi as-Sirhindi ق
26. Muḥammad al-Masum ق
27. Muḥammad Sayfuddin al-Farūqi al-Mujaddidi ق
28. as-Sayyid Nūr Muḥammad al-Badawani ق
29. Shamsuddin Habib Allāh ق
30. ʿAbdAllāh ad-Dahlawi ق
31. Khālid al-Baghdādī ق
32. Ismail Muḥammad ash-Shirwāni ق
33. Khas Muḥammad Shirwāni ق
34. Muḥammad Effendi al-Yaraghi ق
35. Jamāluddin al-Ghumuqi al-Ḥusayni ق
36. Abū Aḥmad as-Sughuri ق
37. Abū Muḥammad al-Madani ق
38. Sharafuddīn ad-Daghestani ق
39. ʿAbdAllāh al-Faʿiz ad-Daghestani
40. Muḥammad Nazim Adil al-Haqqani ق

Recitation Before Every Association

بسم الله الرحمن الرحيم

A'ūdhu billāhi min ash-Shayṭān ir-rajīm.
Bismillāhi' r-Raḥmāni 'r-Raḥīm.
Nawaytu 'l-arbā'īn, nawaytu 'l-'itikāf,
nawaytu'l-khalwah, nawaytu 'l-'uzlah,
nawaytu 'r-riyāḍa, nawaytu 's-sulūk,
lillāhi Ta'alā fī hādhā 'l-masjid.

Ati' ūllāh wa ati' ūr-Rasūl
wa ūli'l-amri minkum.

I seek refuge in Allāh from Satan, the rejected.
In the Name of Allāh, the Merciful,
the Compassionate.
I intend the forty (days of seclusion);
I intend seclusion in the mosque,
I intend seclusion, I intend isolation,
I intend discipline (of the ego); I intend to travel
in God's Path for the sake of God,
in this mosque.

Obey Allāh, obey the Prophet,
and obey those in authority among you.
Sūratu 'n-Nisā (The Women), 4:59

Enter through the Door and Dwell in the City

A'ūdhu billāhi min ash-Shayṭān ir-rajīm. Bismillāhi' r-Raḥmāni 'r-Raḥīm. Nawaytu 'l-arbā'īn, nawaytu 'l-'itikāf, nawaytu'l-khalwah, nawaytu 'l-'uzlah, nawaytu 'r-riyāḍa, nawaytu 's-sulūk, lillāhi Ta'alā fī hādhā 'l-masjid. Ati' ūllāh wa ati'ū 'r-Rasūl wa ūli 'l-amri minkum. (4:59)

Those who are on authority have the key for the door of Prophet ﷺ. To reach the main door, you must go through many doors until you reach the door of that city. Every door has people who are attracted to it, and these are *awlīyāullāh* who receive from Prophet ﷺ, to whom they came through one door, as Prophet ﷺ described:

Anā madinatu 'l-'ilmi wa 'Aliyyun babuha.
I am the city of knowledge and 'Alī is its door. (al-Ḥākim, Tirmidhī)

They enter through that main door and inside they find the one who is with Prophet ﷺ always, who migrated with him from Mecca to Madinah, Sayyīdinā Abu Bakr as-Siddiq ؓ! That means if you want to reach that city it is easy: first use the *dhikrullāh* that Prophet ﷺ showed to Sayyīdinā 'Alī ؓ, described as *"lā ilāha illa-Llāh."* Prophet ﷺ said to 'Alī, "Close your eyes and listen to what I say," and he ﷺ said, *"lā ilāha illa-Llāh,"* three times.

Why three times and not four, or four times and not two? *li-anna Allāhu witrun wa yuhib al-witr.* "Allāh is 'One' and He loves everything to be with odd numbers."

Regarding the recitation of *lā ilāha illa-Llāh* three times, the first recitation is to negate, deny and throw out of the heart everything from *dunya*. You are saying, "*Yā Rabbī*! I am directing myself to You by throwing away *dunya* and coming to You!" The second recitation of *lā ilāha illa-Llāh* means, "I am coming through your beloved, Sayyīdinā Muḥammad ﷺ!" The third recitation of *lā ilāha illa-Llāh* is to come through the door where Sayyīdinā 'Alī is standing. These are the three parts of the key and the code of, "I am the city of knowledge and 'Alī is its door."

When that door opens, that is something else. Like on Hajj, on the day of Arafat before everyone comes, they open *Ka'aba* to wash it and what is inside? That door is the *Ka'aba* that is in everyone's heart, where there are guardians: Sayyīdinā ʿAlī ☀, Sayyīdinā Abu Bakr as-Siddiq ☀, and Sayyīdinā Muḥammad ☀! When you open the first lock, you enter there by the way that Prophet showed Abu Bakr as-Siddiq to come to Allāh ☀ and to him. When you use that word, the door of Prophet opens and from there you begin to see all these manifestations that are inside the *Kaʿaba*. Prophet ☀ said to the *Sahabah* ☀ and to Sayyīdinā ʿAlī ☀ and to all Prophet's *khalīfahs*:

Ma fadalakum abu bakr bi shay'in min ṣalāt wa sawam wa lakin hajattan fi qalbih.
Abu Bakr did not surpass you by offering excessive prayers and fasting, but by 'shay'in waqara fi qalbihi,' something (unique) that entered his deepest, innermost heart.

That is something unique that Abu Bakr ☀ used to approach Prophet ☀ and Allāh ☀, and it distinguished him from others. (Mawlana sneezes.) That sneeze is confirmation of what we are saying, and that Sayyīdinā Abu Bakr as-Siddiq ☀ is looking at us from his place!

So as we said, the Prophet ☀ taught Sayyīdinā ʿAlī ☀ *Dhikr al-Lisān,* "*Dhikr* of the Tongue," by saying *"lā ilāha illa-Llāh,"* and he showed Sayyīdinā Abu Bakr ☀ *Dhikr al-Jinān,* "the Hidden (silent) *Dhikr.*" This hidden *dhikr* is not by tongue, as the tongue is the main door to enter. Then when you enter, you do *dhikrullāh* of *ʿIsm adh-Dhāt,* Allāh's Most Beautiful Name that encompasses all Names, *lafdhatu 'l-Jalālah,* "Allāh."

That is why Allāh ☀ said in Holy Qur'an:

Qul Allāh thumma dharhum fi khawdihim yalʿabūn.
Say, "Allāh," then leave them to play in their vain discussions.

(Sūrat al-ʿAnʿām, 6:91)

SubḥānAllāh! This is a prediction of today's situation and something new coming with Mawlana Shaykh Nazim's *madad.* It was mentioned in the Holy Qur'an 1,400 years ago that there will be people who deny making *dhikr* by *ʿism al-Jalālah.* Just as ignorant people from the time of Prophet ☀ denied the existence of Allāh, there are people today who deny the mention of Allāh in the heart by reciting Allāh's Name; they say it is *bidʿa, kufr, shirk,* and *harām.* Allāh ☀ said to Prophet ☀, "Don't listen to them, but instead say '*Allāh, Allāh,*' as it has been mentioned in Holy Qur'an; say it and don't listen to them."

Why does He want the mention of "Allāh;" why not *"ar-Raḥmān"*, *"ar-Raḥīm,"* *"al-Mālik,"* *"al-Quddūs,"* *"al-Mu'min,"* or *"al-Muhaymin"*? Because Allāh ﷻ manifested upon every prophet one of His Beautiful Names; what He gives to that prophet is under that Divine Name, which He can manifest on many of the 124,000 prophets. But Prophet Muḥammad ﷺ is highest among all prophets, so Allāh gave him the highest Name and manifested Himself to Prophet by that Name. Therefore, all prophets have to be under him and under that Name, "Allāh, The One, Unique." They cannot all be under the same various Divine Names.

Awlīyāullāh are inheritors from prophets, and which prophet they inherit from is based on the manifestations of the Beautiful Names they are under. As long as there are *awlīyā,* there will always be one on top, the Sultan al-Awliya, as Sayyīdinā Muḥīyyidīn ibn ʿArabi ق mentioned. Similarly, for *anbīyā* there is the only one with the station Khatam al-Anbiya, "Seal of Prophets," and Sultan al-Anbiya, "King of Prophets." Prophet ﷺ gets something special in addition to what he has, and he also shares everything he receives with all prophets. Other prophets don't share; each of them is under a private Beautiful Name, but Prophet ﷺ is under *ʿism al-jamiʿ lil-ʿasma wa'ṣ-ṣiffāt.* Allāh ﷻ is manifesting Himself to Prophet ﷺ through His Beautiful Name that encompasses all Beautiful Names and Attributes, "Allāh".

So He said, "Say, *'Allāh'*." Why not say "ar-Raḥmān"? Because ar-Raḥmān is a description, an adjective; "Allāh" is the main Name. He ﷻ said, "Come to Me directly through the Name "Allāh" as there is no obstacle for you, *yā* Muḥammad! All My doors are open to you and I brought you in *Miʿrāj* to dress you with that Name!" The proof that Prophet ﷺ is under that Name is in Holy Qur'an:

> *Wa annahū lamma qāma ʿabdAllāh, yadʿūhū kādū yakūnū ʿalayhi libada.*
> *Yet when the devotee of Allāh stands forth to invoke Him, they just make a dense crowd around him.* (Sūrat al-Jinn, 72:19)

Is there anywhere else where Allāh mentioned Prophet directly as "*ʿabdAllāh*"? That is exclusively for Prophet ﷺ and it means he is the one under the *tajalli* of that Name. As he is under that *tajalli,* how he is going to be called? ʿAbdAllāh, "Servant of Allāh"; that is the real *ʿabd,* the rest are imitations. What is he called, other than *Raḥmatan lil-ʿĀlamīn,* "Mercy to all the Worlds"? Every scholar you ask will say Prophet ﷺ is *al-Insān al-Kāmil,* "the Perfect Human Being." There is no other, there is only one: the Prophet ﷺ *Allāhuma sallī ʿalā Sayyīdinā Muḥammad* ﷺ!

That Beautiful Name has been described:

Qul Huw Allāhu Ahad.
Say (O Muḥammad), "He is 'Allāh', The One, Who has no partner."
(Sūrat al-Ikhlās, 112:1)

Say "Allāh," *qul Huwa,* "The One Who Is completely unknown," Whose reality of that Essence cannot be known, except under the Name, Allāh. All the descriptions from the Beautiful Names and Attributes come under that. But in reality, His Essence, the Absolute Unknown, the Hidden, is "Allāh," and He is "Ahad". "Allāh" is higher than "Ahad," the description. Say, "Allāh, the One with no partner, no child, no description of Him." That is "Allāh".

Wa annahū lamma qāma ʿabdAllāh, yadʿūhū kādū yakūnū ʿalayhi libada, "the One Who is also Unknown," as no one knows the Prophet's ﷺ rank or what Allāh ﷻ gave him. He is known as "The Only (real) ʿAbdAllāh," because the Name "Allāh" means, "The One Who is Absolutely Unknown," so the one who is under that Name is Muḥammad ﷺ, *al-Insān al-Kāmil.*

That Holy Name was put to give The Essence a name, which is "Allāh." But to understand that Name is impossible, so you understand through the other holy descriptions. "Allāh" is described through all the Godly Attributes, *ʿAsma ar-Rubūbiyya,* the Names of Lordship, *al-Jalāl,* "The Majestic," *al-Jamāl,* "The Beauty," and *al-Kamāl,* "The Perfection"; these are descriptions of Allāh ﷻ.

Wa huwa ʿIsmun lidh-Dhāt al-Buht is the Name given to the Secret, the Essence. As close as you zoom in, it is the Name for that Absolute Unknown, *al-ʿAma al-Mutlaq.* No one can see it as it is veiled. Even the Prophet ﷺ cannot see that Essence, although He is under the manifestation of that Name we just described, "Allāh." So the Name "Allāh" is higher than all the Divine Beautiful Names.

That is why Prophet ﷺ is higher than all prophets, as he is carrying the manifestation of that Name, and he is *Raḥmatan lil-ʿĀlamīn.* He was dressed with that Name, and that is why all prophets will come with their nations asking for Prophet's ﷺ mercy, *shafāʿa,* and blessing, because he is under the manifestation of that highest Name which all other Names are under. It is considered in the Islamic Schools of Thought, especially in the Hanafi *madhhab,* that *'Ismullāh al-'Azham* is the Name that Allāh manifested on His Prophet ﷺ.

Sayyīdinā Musa ﷺ asked, "*Yā Rabbī*! Tell me, what is Your Greatest Name? Let me see you. Let me know Your Greatest Name," and all prophets asked that. But Allāh ﷻ said, "O Musa! That is not for you, that is only for My Beloved, Sayyīdinā Muḥammad. So what is for you? Look at the mountain." He sent His manifestation on the mountain and Sayyīdinā Musa fainted, because he had trespassed his limit. In *Mi'rāj,* Sayyīdinā Jibrīl ﷺ said to Prophet ﷺ, "I cannot go further or cross this limit, but you can go further." Sayyīdinā Musa asked to cross the limits, and Allāh taught him a lesson.

> *He said, "O my Lord! Show Yourself to me, that I may look upon You." Allāh said, "By no means can you see Me (directly), but look upon the mountain; if it abides in its place then you shall see Me." When his Lord manifested His glory on the mount, He made it as dust and Moses fell down in a swoon. When he recovered his senses, he said, "Glory be to You! To You I return in repentance, and I am the first to believe."* (Sūrat al-A'rāf, 7:143)

That is when he realized that what he requested from Allāh ﷻ is reserved exclusively for Muḥammad ﷺ!

In his *tafsīr,* Ibn 'Abbas ؓ said, "When Musa fainted, he saw all the prophets in *sajdah,* except for the 313 who were standing in prayer." So it is not a sin for them, but it is a limit not to transgress. Allāh ﷻ is teaching them, "That is reserved for My beloved one, Sayyīdinā Muḥammad!"

According to Sayyīdinā Abu Hanifa an-Nu'man's ؓ *madhhab,* that Name is the exclusive manifestation for Prophet only; no one can share it. That is why he was able to go on *Mi'rāj.* If he was not carrying *'Ismullāh al-'Āzam,* he would have fainted, but because he was carrying that he was able to go through.

Tasbih that Takes You Directly through the Door

So what is our luck? In Naqshbandi Ṭarīqah, our *dhikr* is "Allāh". With that, they take you there directly. As soon as they give you initiation, if that shaykh is real and connected, as soon as you put your hand you enter in that unique area and you are inside! You pass through the door of Sayyīdinā 'Alī ؓ, who says, "He is our guest, let him in." Like with Sayyīdinā

Muḥammad ﷺ when he went in *Mi'rāj* with Jibrīl ﷺ, they knocked on the door at each Heaven, and the angels asked, "Who is with you, Jibrīl?" Sayyīdinā Jibrīl answered, "Muḥammad." Then they asked, "Is he invited?" "Yes," replied Jibrīl. Do you think that angels don't know he is invited? Of course they know, but this is to show more honor. When you take initiation, it means you are invited.

O People! Who are listening or not listening around the world, if you take *baya'* on the Internet or through a representative, that means you have an invitation to enter that city. You then wear a name tag on your chest, a medallion that reads, "Come in, you are invited! *Allāhuma sallī 'alā Sayyīdinā Muḥammad*!

We try to remind ourselves of the person upon whom Allāh manifested the *'Ism adh-Dhāt* by making *dhikr* with the Name "Allāh" as ordered by our shaykh. That Name represents, "The One Who created the perfect servant." When Adam ﷺ was between clay and water, or between body and soul, that is the "perfect human being" who accumulates from the Divine Name, "*al-Jāmi'i,*" which contains *kull al-marātib al-ilāhiyyah,* "all different divine levels."

That is the reality of that perfect human being: he contains the heavenly world, *Malakūt,* and worldly universes, *Mulk,* and carries all universes' secrets, as he is under the *tajallī* of *'Ismullāh al-'Azham.* All minds, souls, and hearts of human beings are under his control, under his keyboard. He can see every one of them by their heavenly name. All universes, worldly and heavenly, are under him. They are created by Allāh ﷻ and are under the blessing of that Name. Prophet ﷺ is *khalīfatullāh fi 'l-mulkih,* "deputy of Allāh among His Creation." So he represents Allāh in every Creation, in Heaven and on Earth.

This might not be even one drop of the ocean of *awlīyāullāh*! We can see how great and strong *awlīyāullāh* are and how weak we are. This will show that we know nothing; the knowledge comes and goes, and we cannot repeat it. These cameras can repeat it, but we cannot. It is in our heart, downloaded, but it needs someone who has the key and is able to upload it.

The heart receives it, but because we are not awake it feels like a dream. Sometimes you remember the dream, sometimes you don't. If you remember, it is good, and if you don't, it is also good, because when they take you to higher levels they close dreams for you. That is good tidings in *ṭarīqah.* As much as you don't know, they keep giving to you in slow doses, but when it becomes a big dose, you might be finished. If they leave you,

you might go crazy, then you would drop everything, and they allow that only for a few people. But for everyone else, if Mawlana Shaykh Nazim ق would open what you have in your heart, you could not bear it and you would run away. You would be in a heavenly coma, always staring at something invisible, no longer "here," so they give it to you slowly.

At the beginning of *ṭarīqah*, they show you so many dreams, then later they stop. What do you want to see dreams for, to grow the ego? They give you dreams in the beginning to attract you, but when you reach the other shore they destroy the boat.

As in Holy Qur'an, when Sayyīdinā Musa was with Khidr ؏ they went in a boat and he made a hole. When it reached the other side it was sinking and therefore the king didn't need it. They take you with your ego to the other side like that boat, but they make a hole and when it reaches the other side the boat begins to sink. That way, you cannot go back! Then they chain you and you become angry, but you have nowhere to run.

So what if the shaykh shouts at you? Keep quiet, don't show him anything now. There is no bridge to bring you back to where you were before. Now you are in the minefield and you have to be clever. They put you in a minefield and say, "Cross it." How will you cross? You need a plan. What is the plan? It is *dhikrullāh*; that will make you cross the minefield! And all of that enters *baytullah*, where people are circumambulating. That *baytullah* in your heart is a duplicate of Ka'abatullah in Mecca.

That is to make sure your home becomes *mazhar tajalliyāt min 'al-'asma wa'ṣ-ṣiffāt*, "the appearance of manifestations of Allāh's Beautiful Names and Attributes." When your heart is like that, it is safe. Allāh's houses are hearts of believers. "Neither Heaven nor Earth contains Me, but the heart of a believer contains Me." Enter your heart, your "inn," then you are safe. Say, "Allāh"! Say, "*Lā ilāha illa-Llāh*!"

May Allāh bless you one by one, and may Mawlana Shaykh be happy with all of you.

Wa min Allāhi 't-tawfīq, bi ḥurmati 'l-ḥabīb, bi ḥurmati 'l-Fātiḥah.
And with Allāh is success. For the sake of the Beloved, for his sake we recite the opening chapter of Holy Qur'an.

Secrets of the Two Oceans

A'ūdhu billāhi min ash-Shayṭān ir-rajīm. Bismillāhi' r-Raḥmāni 'r-Raḥīm. Nawaytu 'l-arbā'īn, nawaytu 'l-'itikāf, nawaytu'l-khalwah, nawaytu 'l-'uzlah, nawaytu 'r-riyāḍa, nawaytu 's-sulūk, lillāhi Ta'alā fī hādhā 'l-masjid. Ati' ūllāh wa ati'ū 'r-Rasūl wa ūli 'l-amri minkum. (4:59)

Allāh ﷻ manifests Himself to all prophets through His Beautiful Names and gave every prophet a way to carry and dress in a different manifestation of His Beautiful Names. Allāh ﷻ manifests Himself on Prophet Muḥammad, the Seal of Messengers ﷺ, through the Name that encompasses all Beautiful Names and Attributes, "Allāh," which is *'Ism adh-Dhāt*. That carries a lot of knowledge to Prophet ﷺ, and under it comes all the different Beautiful Names and Attributes.

How many (Arabic) letters are in "Allāh"? *Alif, lām, lām, hā.* Four is where Allāh ﷻ gave the Prophet ﷺ authority to reach. The heart is of five different spiritual levels, but physically the heart is comprised of four chambers. Every chamber represents one of these letters. *Alif* is the first letter of "Allāh." It represents the secret of *alif* and goes in one chamber. The secret of the next letter, *lam*, goes in another chamber, then *lam* in another chamber, then *ha* in another chamber. That has been given.

The heart has five spiritual levels. The lowest is *Maqām al-Qalb*, and the whole of *dunyā* affairs is there. The second level is "the Level of the Secret," given to all prophets and all *awlīyā* inherited from that *maqām*. That is why *awlīyāullāh* who inherited from different *ṭarīqahs* are in the second level, "the Secret". So the second and third levels merged together. Who wants to come to the Prophet ﷺ must come through that second level, which is the door of Sayyīdinā 'Alī ؓ. If you want to enter the Secret, pass by Sayyīdinā 'Alī ؓ, and there is no other way. And the third level is Sirr as-Sirr, "the Secret of the Secret." There you enter the Name, "Allāh". There are two kinds of *dhikr* of *lā ilāha illa-Llāh*: *ithbāt wa nafiy*, "to affirm and to deny." You affirm "There is no god save Allāh," and you deny everything that is other than Allāh.

Then you are ready to make *dhikr* with *'Ism adh-Dhāt*, the Name that encompasses all Names: "Allāh." That is the *dhikr* Prophet ﷺ taught Sayyīdinā Abū Bakr aṣ-Ṣiddīq ق, and those who took from him are people of the Naqshbandi Ṭarīqah. The two oceans of Sayyīdinā 'Alī ≉ and Sayyīdinā Abū Bakr aṣ-Ṣiddīq ≉ merge, *maraj al-baḥryan*, in Sayyīdinā Jafar aṣ-Ṣiddīq ≉. Then that takes you to the fourth level, *Akhfā*, "the Hidden," which is exclusively for Prophet ≋; no one else can enter there. *Lā sharīk lahu*, in that position there is no associate with Prophet ≋ in his servanthood. The fifth level, *Maqām al-Khafā*, "the Absolute Hidden," is exclusively for Allāh. The *'Amā al-Kāmil* is completely veiled and no one can see anything in that level. So with these four letters of the Name "Allāh," the secret goes into the four chambers of the heart. And as you open it, chamber after chamber you will see what cannot be seen, you will hear what cannot be heard (the *ḥadīth* of Prophet about the Station of Moral Excellence).

When you say "Allāh," you are describing the Essence of Allāh. With the *alif*, you understand it means "the Creator." When you remove the "*alif*," "Allāh" becomes "*lillāh*," *lām-lām-hā*, which means "what belongs to God." It is no longer His Name, but describes what belongs to Him; the Name is gone. What belongs to Him? Everything. But whatever belongs to Him, He gave to you; He is not in need of anything He created, and He gave it to Sayyīdinā Muḥammad ≋. Allāh ≉ is not in need and He created what belongs to Him. So we are subject to Him, not only humans, but everything that is created. People's thinking is limited, so you cannot expand it to see what belongs to Him. This example will show us what belongs to Him, and this is one of the descriptions of *al-Insān al-Kāmil*, "the Perfect Man," (Prophet Muḥammad) who receives all kinds of manifestations.

"O My Lord! Show Me Your Kingdom"

To understand what belongs to Allāh, Sayyīdinā Jibrīl ≋ asked, "*Yā Rabbī!* Can I see Your Kingdom?"

"Yes, why not? No problem." Allāh ≉ loves His servants. "If you want, I will show you. I gave you 600 power engines, turbines, 600 wings."

When he came to Prophet ≋, Jibrīl ≋ used two wings. He came from his place beyond the universe, a heavenly Kingdom, with two wings in less than one second. When Allāh ≉ orders it, it appears. Don't be surprised; that is Allāh! Physicists have calculated the smallest fraction of a second; they found at 10^{-22} of a second, time disappears and only energy remains. So in that fraction of time, energy moves so fast. That is why he was there immediately in front of Prophet ≋.

So he said, "*Yā Rabbī*! Show me Your Kingdom."

"I will show you, but why, don't you believe?"

"It's not that, but it is to make my heart content."

Behold! Abraham said, "My Lord! Show me how You give life to the dead." He said, "Do you not believe?" He said, "Yes (I believe), but to satisfy My own understanding." He said, "Take four birds, tame them to turn to you, put a portion of them on every hill and call them. They will come to you (flying) with speed. Then know that Allāh is Exalted in Power, Wise." (Sūrat al-Baqarah, 2:260)

Sayyīdinā Ibrāhīm ﷺ said, "O Allāh! Show me how You create."

"Why do you want to know that?"

"How do You create?"

The *anbīyā* want to teach us, so they ask, but Prophet Muḥammad ﷺ never asked.

So Allāh ﷻ said, "You don't believe I can create?"

Sayyīdinā Ibrāhīm ﷺ was afraid then; how had he dared to ask that question? But he could not take it back. It is like on a computer when you write a text message or email, you press "send" and after you send it, it is gone. In the past you would write a letter, but before you sent it, it would take time and you might change your mind about what you wrote. But on the computer you send it, and you cannot bring it back. So be careful what you write. And be careful with Facebook! It is the worst thing, teaching people bad character. Allāh ﷻ and Prophet ﷺ and *awlīyā* are not happy with Facebook. Close your Facebook account!

So Allāh ﷻ said, *awalam tu'min,*, "Do you not believe?" Ibrāhīm answered, "No, it is not that, but I am asking so my heart will be content."

"What Ibrāhīm? Your heart is not content?"

He said, "Show me how You create, as I want my heart to be content."

Sayyīdinā Muḥammad ﷺ never asked, because his heart is always content.

Allāh ﷻ said, "Okay, you are My *khalīfah* on Earth, so I will show you. Take a bird, cut it into pieces and put them on four hills and then call those pieces. They will come together and they will come running to you!"

Allāh ﷻ is the Creator. So when Jibrīl ﷺ asked, "Can I see Your Kingdom, *yā Rabbī*?" Allāh ﷻ said, "Okay," since Jibrīl ﷺ also wanted contentment, to see how big this universe is. And Allāh ﷻ ordered him to use his 600 wings, not to use two wings. Through this universe, he was appearing in less than a moment with two wings. What do you think about him using those 600 wings, or turbines? Allāh ﷻ knows what they are, these heavenly wings, or turbines, to move in space, able to see Allāh's Kingdom. By that order he was moving. Imagine how much he could move and see in one moment! Can we calculate that to see how big is Allāh's Kingdom? No. Allāh's Kingdom is not this Earth, according to the *hadīth*:

> *Law kānati 'd-dunyā tazin 'indallāhi janāḥa ba'ūda mā saqā kāfir minhā shurbatu māi.*

It means, "In Allāh's Sight, the value of this world is less than the wing of a mosquito." And Jibrīl moved, moved, moved by Allāh's order until he became exhausted. Do angels get exhausted? No. So why did he? Because this Kingdom was beyond his power, beyond his 600 wings.

He told Allāh, "This Kingdom is so big it is beyond me! Is there still more?"

"*Yā* Jibrīl, what do you mean, 'still more'? You didn't move around a corner yet!"

He moved non-stop for 70,000 years and he got tired. That is why human beings get tired after they grow old. If Jibrīl ﷺ didn't get tired, then human beings would not get tired and you would have long life; that reflection came on this Creation.

And he said, "Is there still more?"

"What you did is nothing, not even an epsilon."

He was so small and it was 70,000 years! And what he saw in that moving was indescribable, with no beginning and no end. It was straight and flat, and we can call it an ocean, full of very small white crystals. Like when you go to the beach and you see white sand, to us there is no beginning and no end and you cannot count how many crystals of sand there are.

Through his power, Sayyīdinā Jibrīl ﷺ was not moving around a corner after 70,000 years of flying, and he saw transparent white crystals without end. They cannot be described, and they were where he was. And in the middle of this was a tree and on it was one green bird that went down, took one crystal in his beak, went up the tree, slowly ate it and swallowed it. And then again went down, picked up another crystal, went up the tree, ate it, and swallowed it, and repeated that again and again.

Jibrīl said, "*Yā Rabbī.* I didn't see anything except this ocean of crystals."
And Allāh ﷻ said, "*Yā* Jibrīl, every *dharrah*, atom, of that crystal is a universe by itself." If Allāh ﷻ can make the Earth go through the eye of a needle without making the needle bigger or making the Earth smaller, can't Allāh then make each crystal a universe?

He said, "So what is that bird?"

"*Yā* Jibrīl, that bird is My beloved, who is ordered to go down and pick up one crystal and swallow it. As soon as it is swallowed, that is an indication that he is *khalīfatullāh* in that *Mulk* and *Malakūt*, in Earth and Heaven, and as soon as he takes that crystal, that universe is created within him, not outside of him."

So that is why all prophets, from Adam ﷺ until the Day of Judgment, come to Prophet ﷺ for *shafā'* on Judgment Day. They are within him, so how will Allāh ﷻ send anyone to Hellfire when they are within Prophet ﷺ?

W 'allamū anna fīkum rasūlullāh.
And know that Prophet is within you. (Sūrat al-Ḥujurāt, 49:7)

Since he is within you, you are within him. And every time he swallows one crystal, that is one Creation, and Prophet ﷺ is Allāh's representative for that Creation, as Muḥammad ﷺ is His Messenger. That is the Perfect Human Being, *al-Insān al-Kāmil.*

Wa laqad karamnā Banī Adam.
We have honored the Children of Adam. (Sūrat al-Isrā', 17:70)

That means no Creation is honored more than human beings. Even angels are not honored as human beings are honored. All that is because of Sayyīdinā Muḥammad ﷺ, who is encompassing all the heavenly and Godly levels. And he is the one who overtakes all the souls of human beings in him. Allāh ﷻ gave him that authority to reach anyone. Previously, the idea of reaching anyone was not understood, but now it is easy to understand through technology. You can reach anyone, you can send an email to anyone. If a server can reach thousands and thousands through networking, can't Prophet ﷺ have a heavenly server to connect with all of humanity? But what do you need to do? You need to reply. If you don't reply, you are the loser. He is ready; his heart is open but you have to go there.

Hūwa al-Jāmiʿ lil marātib al-ilāhīyya min al-ʿuqūl wa 'n-nufūs al-kullīya wa 'l-juzī'yyah. He is "the One that Contains." "Al-Jāmiʿ" accumulates, collects, contains *marātib al-ilāhīyya,* all the Godly stations Allāh ﷻ gave him. He has already grasped or overtaken and encompassed every Godly station in the Heavens and the angelic world, and it is under his command; not only the Godly stations, but *kawnīyya* also. Whatever is in this universe is under him and, not only that, all brains, *min al-ʿuqūl.* That means in every brain there is a chip that is smaller than a lentil, filled with intelligence. It means that chip is connected to him, to that server. *Wa 'n-nufūs,* the selves, all people's selves are in his hands, *al-kullīya wa 'l-juzī'yyah,* all of it, even the smallest particle of it. That is why he is *khalīfatullāh.*

Innī jaʿilun fi 'l-arḍi khalīfah.
I will create a vicegerent on Earth. (Sūrat al-Baqarah, 2:30)

Under him is all Creation until there will be no more Creation. It is impossible, as creation is continuous, because Allāh is the Creator, "al-Khāliq." So every moment Creation is under the control of Prophet ﷺ. This level is called *al-Martabat al-ʿAmīyya,* "the Level of Blindness," not in the meaning of physical blindness, but meaning that the only one who can reach that level and see it is Prophet ﷺ; anyone else is blind and cannot see it. *Wa li-dhālika sār khalīfatullāh.* For that reason he became a *khalīfah,* representative, of Allāh ﷻ. That is why from the beginning Allāh ﷻ put his name with His Own, *Lā ilāha illa-Llāh Muḥammadun Rasūlullāh.*

There is no other who was raised as the Prophet ﷺ was, and that is why he has control over the heart. When we say "Allāh," *alif* represents the Name of the Essence which no one can know. *Qūl Hūw Allāh.* "Say, the One (Who was unknown) is Named 'Allāh'." If you take away the *alif,* it represents all that belongs to Him, *lillāh.* If you take the next *lam* it is *lahu;* that means no one can share anything with Him. You cannot say, "I am partner." Everything *lahu,* you cannot touch it. And if you take next *lam* it is *huw,* the Absolute Unknown. Those four letters have been given to Prophet ﷺ, who represents *ʿIsmullāh al-ʿAẓam.*

And as Sayyīdinā Abū Hanīfa ؓ said, "That Name, "Allāh," is given to Prophet ﷺ and with it you can say to a thing, *kun fayakūn,* "'Be!' and it will be." (36:82)

According to Grandshaykh ق, that Name has been given to Prophet ﷺ in the beginning of every *sūrah*. So that is why he has given me this notebook of his shaykh, Shaykh Sharafuddīn ق, written in very beautiful calligraphy that I copied by hand, as there were no copying machines at that time. It contains the first verses of each *sūrah,* so if you read these first verses of each chapter, you are passing by Allāh's Greatest Name but you don't know what it is. That is why it is recommended to read it. We can write it and pass it to people. Sometimes it is one verse (*awail as-sūr*) and sometimes it is two. So that has been given to Prophet ﷺ.

Shaykh Aḥmad al-Fārūqī al-Sirhindī ق said that on the journey of seekers in our Way, the Naqshbandi Order, "When the seeker in our *ṭarīqah* is not busy with *dunyā* matters, we will make him busy with heavenly matters." It means stop running after *dunyā,* because *dunyā* makes you a slave to it and you must make *dunyā* a slave for you.

The *awlīyā* give everything to Allāh ﷻ; they have no privacy and their life is "hacked"; everyone can enter and see what they are doing. So Shaykh Aḥmad al-Faruqi said, "If they are not busy in *dunyā* work we will give them heavenly work by making them *nushghilahum bi wuqūf al-qalbi,* 'always alert in their heart,' preparing them to enter the Divine Presence through what we teach them, through *at-tawajjuh.*" This is how to prepare themselves, to direct themselves to enter the reality of the human soul's secret, *ar-Rūh al-Insāni.* The human *Rūh* is not only the soul, but the inner soul of the soul. "We will show them how they can begin their journey within their own self."

Doctors today are mostly spies of the human body, where there is a sickness. They write what this one has and they make a big file about your health. *Awlīyā* are spies of the heart and doctors are spies of the body. This is especially true with the MRI today, when they put you in something like a coffin. You have to remember death, when you will be confined in a box. *Awlīyāullāh* have an MRI machine. Is there a more advanced machine? Not yet. *Awlīyāullāh* have a more advanced machine for what they detect, the *Rūh al-Insāni,* the soul of the soul. The doctors go through your whole body to eliminate all that is not needed, and similarly, to receive these beautiful manifestations of Allāh's Beautiful Names and Attributes, you have to go through the heart, *wuqūf qalbī.*

It is through that *wuqūf,* not through beads or anything. When they see you are not interested in *dunyā* life they put you directly on that journey. The *qalb* is the door of the inner soul, of the human soul. At the beginning, that inner soul of the human soul is inside the body. The *rūh* is in the prison of the body, the cage, but its life is connected through the heart. If the heart stops pumping, finished. So the heart is the controller of the inner soul, to keep it. When the heart is able to expand and the door is opened, it will set free your inner soul. When the inner soul of the soul is freed, then the soul is able to move everywhere within your self and it comes to know the inner self.

That is why Prophet ﷺ said:

Man ʿarafa nafsahu faqad ʿarafa Rabbahu.
Who knows his self knows his Lord.

So what do you know about yourself? Only your mistakes? No, Allāh ﷻ doesn't care about that! He wants to show you His mercy, and to show you Sayyīdinā Muḥammad ﷺ is in everyone's heart and body. He wants to show you His Light in you!

Allāhu Nūr as-samawāti wal-ʿarḍ.
Allāh is the Light of the Heavens and Earth. (Sūrat an-Nūr, 24:35)

Allāh ﷻ said to Prophet ﷺ directly in a *Ḥadīth Qudsī*:

Ma wasiʿanī arḍī wa lā samāʾī wa lākin wasiʿanī qalbi ʿabdī al-muʾmin.
My Earth did not contain Me, nor My Heavens, but the heart of My believing servant contained Me.

It means Allāh ﷻ is the heart of the *nūr* in every person. Allāh's Light shines in you! So you, O ignorant one, you dumb one! Do you think Allāh's Light is not in you? They are there, waiting for it to be given. Allāh ﷻ doesn't look at dirtiness, but He looks at everything *jamīlah*, beautiful. That is why He said:

Wa laqad karamnā Banī Adam.
We have honored the sons of Adam. (Sūrat al-Isrāʿ, 17:70)

"We have honored human beings with *anwārullāh*, Allāh's Lights." Everyone has different lights and he is known by these lights to Prophet ﷺ, and not one resembles the other light, no way. So imagine what endless oceans of light have been dressed on human beings, the Perfect Creation. And at that time, Allāh ﷻ wants you to know, He will see that *ʿabd* and He will see the light of his soul and the perfection of his self, because this is the work that Prophet ﷺ is assigning, *man ʿarifa nafsahu faqad ʿarifa rabbah.*

That is why Allāh ﷻ is assigning helpers in your soul, to help you know yourself and your divine lights. The saying is not, "To know the badness of yourself, then you know your Lord." No, you must know the lights of your Lord inside you, then you know your reality in the Divine Presence. Everyone has a reality in the Divine Presence. You are connected with that reality, and this here is a copy of reality that is there. That came on the Day of Promises when Allāh ﷻ asked, "Am I not your Lord?" and everyone said, "Yes You are, *yā Rabbī*!" Even Iblīs knows his Lord, but he is cursed.

At that time you will know the reality and then you will be guided to *maʿrifatullāh* through these lights, to know about your Creator and what you can carry, what you can take. *Wa yukāshif asrārihi wa asmā'ihi Taʿalā*, "He will discover Allāh's Beautiful Names and Attributes in everything around him." He will know every secret of every tree, every herb and in everything that is created in humans or animal or nature, and will be able to know what every atom has been created for and what is its *taṣbīḥ*. That's why he says, *man kashafa ʿanhu anwār nafsihi yankhashif ʿanhu asrāra rabbih.* "Who discovers or uncovers the light of his self will uncover the light of his Lord's secret."

May Allāh ﷻ forgive us and may Allāh ﷻ bless us.

Wa min Allāhi 't-tawfiq, bi ḥurmati 'l-ḥabīb, bi ḥurmati 'l-Fātiḥah.

And with Allāh is success. For the sake of the Beloved, for his sake we recite the opening chapter of Holy Qur'an.

Levels and Rewards of the Highest Character

A'ūdhu billāhi min ash-Shayṭān ir-rajīm. Bismillāhi' r-Raḥmāni 'r-Raḥīm. Nawaytu 'l-arbā'īn, nawaytu 'l-'itikāf, nawaytu'l-khalwah, nawaytu 'l-'uzlah, nawaytu 'r-riyāḍa, nawaytu 's-sulūk, lillāhi Ta'alā fī hādhā 'l-masjid. Ati' ūllāh wa ati'ū 'r-Rasūl wa ūli 'l-amri minkum. (4:59)

As we mentioned, the Prophet ﷺ is "the Perfect Human Being," *al-Insān al-Kāmil*, as it is mentioned in the *Tawrāt* that Allāh created human beings on *sūratih*, His Own Image. Okay, we understand that (*sūrah*) is more symbolic, but it means Allāh ﷻ reflected and manifested the continuous spring of His Beautiful Names and Attributes that have no end on the Prophet ﷺ.. Every moment a spring is coming; not just one spring, but springs are coming like fountains of water describing the reality of the Essence that cannot be understood, except through that one who is reflecting it to us, "*al-Insān al-Kāmil*."

He is the one receiving these blessings or manifestations and reflecting them to all Creation. The only one who can receive that is Prophet ﷺ, the Perfect Human Being. It is said that he is the mirror on which Allāh ﷻ reflects Himself. He sends those images or realities, and the mirror, Insān al-Kāmil, reflects them on anyone in the Heavens or Earth who needs them.

That is why Sayyīdinā Muḥīyyidīn ibn 'Arabi ؓ said, "The Prophet is the mirror of the Divine Presence." And he said more than that, he went so deep. "If Allāh wants to look at His Creation, he looks at His mirror, the Prophet ﷺ, who is the reflection of these appearances in this Universe." I hope we understood? That is why it is said the *ghawth* receives directly from the Prophet and then he sends on to those five *quṭbs* who are waiting for these manifestations. That is why it is said that one who has *qatratun*, one drop, is:

'Aynun fīha tusamma Salsabīlah.
A fountain there called, "Salsabīl." (Sūrat al-'Insān, 76:18)

That mirror reflects a spring mentioned in *Sūrat al-Insān* as *'aynun fīha tusamma Salsabīlah*, "It is a spring called '*Salsabīl*'." It is a knowledge that never ends, and who is able to drink even one drop from that spring will become a servant of Allāh. That is why Sayyīdinā al-Khiḍr was able to drink from that *mā' al-hayyāt*, the "Fountain of Youth," but in reality, in Heavens it is called the "Spring of *Salsabīl*."

Salsabīl quenches the thirst of *'ibādAllāh* whom Allāh dressed with that. It is said they understand the reality of *al-Insān al-Kāmil* through his best character as he must possess that.

> *Nūn wa al-qalami wa mā yasṭurūna mā anta bini'mati rabbika bi-majnūnin wa inna laka la-ajran ghayra mamnūnin wa innaka la-'alā khuluqin 'aẓīm.*
>
> *Nūn. By the Pen and what the (angels) write. You (O Muḥammad) are not, by the Grace of your Lord, a madman. And verily, for you will be an endless reward, and verily, you are on an exalted standard of character.*
>
> (Sūrat al-Qalam, 68:1-4)

Allāh gives an oath by the Arabic letter, "*nūn*," and what is *nūn*? Allāh knows best, but we will explain this once. "*Nūn*" is the highest heavenly level by which Allāh gives an oath, that, "Yā Muḥammad! You are of the best character!" From it *'ibādAllāh* are quenching their thirst, those who want to understand and become deeply involved in these fountains, and to reach *taḥaqquq*, Certainty. That is why it is said, *man taḥaqqaqa takhalaqa*, "Who reached (the Station of) Certainty, Allāh will dress with best character."

So if you wish to reach best character, you must reach the Stations of Certainty: *'Ilm al-Yaqīn*, "Knowledge of Certainty," *'Ayn al-Yaqīn*, "Vision of Certainty," and *Ḥaqq al-Yaqīn*, "Truth of Certainty."

Muḥīyyidīn ibn 'Arabi ❧ continues, "Whoever inherits from that will have perfect character. Any appearance from what Allāh creates can appear only through the mirror of the Prophet ❧." *Wa man takhalaqa taḥaqqaqa*, "Who inherits from the Prophet of good character will become certain of what he is hearing and seeing."

So if we want to reach the Station of Certainty, we need to reach good character. Do we have good character? (No.) Do you shout at your wife? (Sometimes.) So the best character is to be patient. Like the ocean, that never complains. If all the sewers go into the ocean, does it complain? No. And it is still clean, you can still make *wuḍū* in it. And if you put filth in any moving river you can still make *wuḍū* in it. So, who reaches the Station of Certainty, his character will be perfected. And whose character is perfected will be stamped, "He reached reality." *man takhalaqa tamazzaq*, "Who reached the best of character and these manifestations will be torn into pieces!"

The Prophet ﷺ is of the best character, and in *dunyā* the he said, "I am the one most abused," *tamazzaqa fi 'l-ḥaqq*, "torn apart in truth." Who wants to reach the best character has to know that in front of him are torture and obstacles, because he knows the truth is there and he is not able to reach the Divine Presence easily. There are countless obstacles he or she has to overcome, *wa man takhalaqa tamazzaqa fil-ḥaqq*. Who has good character will be torn to pieces in the reality, the truth. And that is why *awlīyāullāh* suffered a lot to reach realities, and their life is filled with obstacles.

Al-Jilī ق, a big scholar and also a *walī*, said, *Istādhir dhi'nuka*, "Focus your mind on us; *mushattat al-afkār*, don't be distracted too much by your thoughts. Open your ears and bring your mind and your heart to focus."

Kullul-aʿrifin al-muwajihīn min al-ḥaqq, "Gnostics crowned with the crown of *maʿrifah* never behaved in the perfect Heavenly Kingdom of Allāh ﷻ except with the best of their characters." So don't lose that. These are the levels of *aqṭāb*, the five *quṭbs*, who are in that level of perfection where they inherit from the Prophet ﷺ. That is why it is said that *al-Insān al-Kāmil* is always in connection with Allāh's Beautiful Names and Attributes that appear to him, and *awlīyā* cannot count how many Beautiful Names and Attributes appear in every moment.

Qul Allāh thumma dharhum fi khawdihim yalʿabūn.
Say, "Allāh," then leave them to play in their vain discussions.
(Sūrat al-'Anʿām, 6:91)

Allāhu Akbar! Say "Allāh," and don't mind about what they are playing; leave *khalq*, human beings/Creation and their affairs. Don't go to their level, as you are in that high level, saying, "Allāh," which is the highest Beautiful Name, that all other Names are under! Mention His Name! That is the source of all Beautiful Names and Attributes sent to Muḥammad ﷺ! So, *inna Allāh wa malā'ikatahu yuṣsallūn*, means Allāh is ordering His angels to carry the manifestations of these Beautiful Names and Attributes that are appearing in every moment, and to dress them on the Prophet. And according to *awlīyā* there is no limit to the Beautiful Names and Attributes manifested on him! It is continuous *khalq*, Creation manifested on the Prophet ﷺ!

It is also said that everyone is dressed with the *tajallī* of one of the Beautiful Names, and Prophet sees you under that *tajallī* and he gives you a name according to that Name, which he knows from the light appears in the divine mirror. As we said but didn't discuss, there is "ʿAbdur-Raḥmān,

'Abdur-Raḥīm, 'Abdul-Ghaffar." Whoever has those names are under the *tajallī* and servanthood of those Beautiful Names. There can be many people having the same name, but each is in a different light, because one Beautiful Name has an infinite number of *tajallīyāt*. That is why we appear with that *tajallī*, our appearance is with the blessing of that light, and when *awlīyā* look at their followers they look at them under that light. They know their rank in the Divine Presence based on the light coming on them. And that is why Prophet is always in connection with the Beautiful Names and Attributes that can be envisioned and seen, and they are the real appearances of Allāh ﷻ on His Prophet ﷺ.

To understand that, you have to carry the best of characters. It is said that the best characters are an infinite number, but what some *awlīyā* counted are about one-thousand good characters. One *walī* who counted around one-thousand good characters said, "Allāh knows best how many there are, and Prophet said, *Anna aḥabakum ilayya wa aqrabakum majlisan akramakum akhlāqan,* 'The one who will sit beside me on Judgment Day is the one with the best manners.'"

And we lack these good manners. Muḥīyyidīn ibn 'Arabi ؓ continues, "Some of these are *al-hilm,* forbearance, *'ilm,* knowledge, to have humility and compassion, and *bashasha,* to be always smiling and friendly in companionship, and *al-'afūw,* to forgive, and *al-iḥsān,* to be generous to the one who harmed you, and to connect to the one who left you, *wa raḥmāh li 'd-du'āfa,* to have mercy on weak people, and *tawqīr mashaykh,* to respect shaykhs." Who respects shaykhs anymore? They don't call themselves shaykhs any more, they call themselves 'doctors.' "And *al-ikhwān,* brotherhood, *wa 's-sabr,* patience, *wa 'z-zuhd,* asceticism, *qana'a, ridā, shukr,* to be thankful..." and it goes on.

Fa lā bud min as-sālik ḥattā yatakhalaq bi-hadhihi 'l-akhlāq, "For the seeker it is essential to attain all these good characters in his journey and not to be tough, but to be a real seeker." Today they say, "We are in *ṭarīqah,*" any *ṭarīqah,* but are they really doing what *ṭarīqah* calls for? Any *ṭarīqah* calls for good character, that is why *mujahad* is not easy. That's why they send you to seclusion, for forty days, six months, one year, one after another, until they crush you completely, until you have good characteristics. When you enter seclusion it is not simple and you are always thinking about when are you coming out, counting the days.

They say, *ṣāḥib ḥusn al-khuluq la-wusil ṣāḥib aṣ-ṣawmi wa 'ṣ-ṣalāt,* "That one who has good character will be raised to the level of the one who is praying and fasting all the time."

Khudh il-ʿawfu w'amr bi'l-ʿurfi wʿarid ʿan il-jāhilīn.

Hold to forgiveness, command what is right, but turn away from the ignorant.

(Sūrat al-Aʿrāf, 7:199)

Be a forgiving person. Don't be like one who cursed you; say, "*Alḥamdulillāh,* he saved me.'" If someone cursed you, especially on the Internet, the least they do for you is to carry your sins! So what should you do? Forgive them, because they made something good for you, they took away all your sins. So what do you have to do? Pray for them, "Yā *Rabbī,* forgive them!" Be happy when they curse you, and don't be happy when they pet you. When they curse you Allāh and Prophet are looking at how are you going to react. Yesterday we had an example: there were two big *murīds* going to the food, and one blocked the way for the other. I was looking to see what he is going to do, as he was blocking the way of the other, who was patient and passed the test.

So, it is said, *al-khuluq afḍal manāqib al-ʿubūdīyya,* "The best character is the best of worship. It will take you to the highest level of Certainty," and realities that we mentioned before. That is why in Holy Qurʿan, Allāh mentioned him as of the best character:

wa 'innaka laʿalā khuluqin ʿaẓīm.
Indeed you are of a tremendous character! (Sūrat al-Qalam, 68:4)

The Prophet ﷺ passed through all of the earthly kingdoms and all the heavenly kingdoms, and reached *fa kāna qāba qawsayni aw adnā,* "within two bows' length or nearer," (53:9) where no one can reach except a perfect one! And they are pure like angels, but even Jibrīl stopped, saying, "I cannot go further, you go!" With this Allāh showed the angels the high level of Sayyīdinā Muḥammad ﷺ. That is why Allāh said:

Yā ayyuha 'l-mudaththir qum fa andhir wa thīyābaka fa-ṭāhhir.
O you (Yā Muḥammad), who covers himself with blankets! Arise and warn, and magnify your Lord, and purify your garments!

(Sūrat al-Mudaththir, 74:1-4)

Prophet ﷺ was sick and covering himself, and here Allāh ﷻ was telling him, "No, in My Kingdom, shivering or not, someone has to keep moving, *qum fa andhir wa rabbuka fa-kabbir,* so wake up and warn people to say, '*Allāhu Akbar, Allāhu Akbar, Allāhu Akbar*! Allāh is Greatest and there is no resemblance to His Greatness.' Tell them to leave their bad characters. Warn them that there is a measure and a balance."

Wa 's-samā rafʿahā wa waḍaʿ al-mīzān.
He raised high the Heavens and put a balance. (Sūrat ar-Raḥmān, 55:7)

To Be an Immigrant in Allāh's Way

Allāh ﷻ raised Heavens and put the Balance, so don't try to transgress it by being a tyrant: balance your *ʿamal*, your ego, your selfishness, and your sins well. That is why He said, *qum fa andhur*, "stand and warn them," then tell them, *Allāhu Akbar, wa rabbuka fa-kabbir*. "Say, '*Allāhu Akbar*,'" one hundred times daily. At that time comes: *wa thīyābak fa-ṭāhhir* , "clean your clothes." Not the normal clothes, but the clothes of the self, as it takes away the bad characters and puts the best characters. There are a thousand good characteristics that we cannot mention them all here, but let them carry these characteristics, *war-rujza fahjur*. "Leave the bad behind, migrate away from it, be an immigrant in Allāh's Way and don't look back at this worldly life, look at the heavenly life." Those are four verses from *Sūrat al-Mudaththir*. And the Prophet ﷺ said:

Wa inna al-ʿabdu yablugha bi ḥusni khuluqihi darajāt aṣ-ṣā'im al-qā'im.
The servant of Allāh will reach with his good character and behaviors.
(Tirmidhī)

Even if he is making sins, if he can give one good character, Allāh will reward him like He rewards the one who is fasting and standing in prayer excessively, doing *nawāfil*, supererogatory, fasts and prayers. That doesn't mean that you can then leave fasting; you have to fast Ramadan, but it means Allāh will reward the one of good character like them. Look how easy it is. You cannot have the good character to smile in the face of others? Like this *murīd*, the other one was blocking him from food last night and he smiled; he showed good character, and that was enough for Allāh to accept all his fasts. And the other one Allāh accepted his fast as He used him to try this one!

Prophet ﷺ said:

Afdal al-mu'minīna imānan ahsanahum khuluqan.
The believers with the best faith are those with the best character. (Bayhaqi)

So let us see how much we have to balance. *Wa wada' al-mīzān.* Balance yourself now. We find ourselves a complete failure. Allāh ﷻ said in Holy Qur'an:

Qālati 'l-'arābū āmanā. Qul lam tu'uminū wa lākin qūlū aslamnā wa lammā yadkhuli 'l-īmānu fi qulūbikum.
The desert Arabs say, "We believe." Say, "You have no faith, but say, 'We have submitted our wills to Allāh,' for not yet has faith entered your hearts."
(Sūrat al-Ḥujurāt, 49:14)

Don't say, "We are *mu'min,*" but say, "We are Muslim," because *imān* did not yet enter the heart.

Prophet ﷺ said:

Wa qāla khuṣlatān la yajtami'ān fi mu'min: al-bukhl wa sūw al-khuluq.
There are two things that cannot be found in a believer: stinginess, and al-khuluq as-sayyī'āt, to carry bad character.

Especially today, people are not concerned with anything. They are carrying bad characteristics; they get angry and they never smile in your face all your life. It is finished, as if mercy disappeared from their hearts. *Wa qāla dhun-nūn, akthar an-nāsu hamman aswāhum khuluqun,* Dhul-Nun said, "Those with the most problems are the ones with bad characteristics." Because of their bad characteristics they always go into problems, and their bad characteristics are reflected in their children. If their parents have good character you see the children are raised nicely, with good discipline. And we ask Allāh to give us good character and to take away our bad dresses!

May Allāh ﷻ forgive us and may Allāh ﷻ bless us.

Wa min Allāhi 't-tawfiq, bi ḥurmati 'l-ḥabīb, bi ḥurmati 'l-Fātiḥah.
And with Allāh is success. For the sake of the Beloved, for his sake we recite the opening chapter of Holy Qur'an.

Examples of the High Character and Forbearance of Awliyaullah

A'ūdhu billāhi min ash-Shayṭān ir-rajīm. Bismillāhi' r-Raḥmāni 'r-Raḥīm. Nawaytu 'l-arbā'īn, nawaytu 'l-'itikāf, nawaytu'l-khalwah, nawaytu 'l-'uzlah, nawaytu 'r-riyāḍa, nawaytu 's-sulūk, lillāhi Ta'alā fī hādhā 'l-masjid. Ati' ūllāh wa ati'ū 'r-Rasūl wa ūli 'l-amri minkum. (4:59)

We have discussed the good character, *al-khuluq al-hasan* and the *ayāt*, "O you, wrapped up (in the mantle)! Arise and deliver your warning! And magnify your Lord! And purify your garments!" (74:1-4) Allāh ﷻ is instructing Prophet ﷺ, "*Yā* Muḥammad! Leave the bed." That means, "Leave *dunyā*, and what makes you feel good."

When people want to feel good and relax, they go to bed to lay down, saying, "I am tired." *Ḥusn al-khuluq*, good character, is when you are tired, you must drop your *nafs* that wants to relax and do something for the benefit of all humanity. So Allāh ﷻ is saying to Prophet ﷺ, "*Yā* Muḥammad, leave the bed. *Qum*, wake up and warn, *andhir*." Warn who? For Prophet, it means warn the *ummah*. But for us there is another interpretation, as Sufism is a taste and *awlīyāullāh* find ways to interpret Holy Qur'an's verses.

> *Wa mā ya'lamū tāwīlahu illa-Llāh war-rāsikhūna fil-'ilmi yaqūlūna āmana bihi kullun min 'indi rabbinā wa mā yadhadhakkarū illa ūlūl-albāb.*
> *But no one knows its hidden meanings except Allāh. And those who are firmly grounded in knowledge say, "We believe in the Book; the whole of it is from our Lord." And none will grasp the Message except men of understanding.*
> (Sūrat 'Āli 'Imrān, 3:7)

No one knows its interpretation except Allāh. *wa 'r-rāsikhūna fil 'ilmi yaqūlūna āmāna*. Those who are like mountains are strong; even a huge tornado cannot do anything to a mountain. It might take the forest, the trees, but the mountain is *rāsikh*, well established on Earth. He didn't say *'ulamā*. So those who are like a mountain of knowledge in religion, not Sharī'ah, say *āmanā*, "we believe," *sami'nā wa at'anā*. We believe that no one knows the interpretation except for Allāh ﷻ, but He gave Prophet ﷺ the Knowledge of Firsts and Lasts (before and after), which means He didn't hide that interpretation from the Prophet ﷺ. That is why Grandshaykh ق told us that Sayyīdinā Mahdī ﷺ will bring the interpretation of every verse and every letter.

"Those who are well established in knowledge, say, 'We believe, everything is from Allāh ﷻ'". But if we read the verse in a different way, *wa mā ya'lamūna tāwīlahu illa-Llāh wa 'r-rāsikhūn fi 'l-'ilm,* in this reading, "No one knows its interpretation except Allāh and those whom Allāh made like mountains, well established." It is *waw 'ataf* from the first part of the word to the second word. *Wa ar-rāsikhūn,* Allāh and those who are well established in knowledge of the Holy Qur'an.

> *Yā ayyuha 'l-mudaththir qum fa andhir wa thīyābaka fa-ṭāhhir.*
> *O you (Yā Muḥammad), who covers himself with blankets! Arise and warn, and magnify your Lord, and purify your garments!*
> (Sūrat al-Muddaththir, 74:1-4)

Warn Your Ego of Harmful Characters and Desires

Yā ayyuha 'l-mudaththir, "Stand up and be ready to warn the *ummah,*" and everyone must warn themselves, their ego. Get up to warn people and for people to warn their egos. How did *awlīyā* become perfected? By warning their egos. *Wa thīyābak fa-ṭāhhir,* "And make your character the best." Tell them to be of best character. If they can be of best character, then they have achieved a lot. Because a best character is to perfect oneself.

At the beginning of Ramadan, we spoke about the five *quṭbs* (poles): *Quṭb, Quṭbu'l Bilād, Quṭbu'l Irshad, Quṭbu'l Aqtab,* and *Quṭbu'l Mutaṣarrif.* We also spoke about the five different groups of *awlīyā: Budalā, Nujabā, Nuqabā, Awtād,* and *Akhyār.* Above all of them is the *Ghawth,* and under them, 124,000 saints. All of them have *khuluq al-hasan.* All that we were discussing from the beginning of Ramadan was to show that *awlīyāullāh* have achieved these high characters and became *rāsikhūn fil-'ilm,* "well established in high levels." Everyone, according to their group and level, has become well established in the Divine Presence. We didn't yet go into their names and what Allāh manifested on them, or what they represent!

So the best of us is the one with the best character. Allāh said to Prophet ﷺ, *wa thīyābak fa-ṭāhhir* , "Purify that dress." That is a *khitāb* to all humanity to purify your clothes, your character. *War-rujzu fahjur,* "Migrate and come out the bad characters." That is why in Arabic, every word in the Holy Qur'an has many meanings. *Fahjurhuna fil-madajia'*, "Let them get a way to come out for men and women." *Fahjur* means "get out of it," don't be completely dipped in the well of Shayṭān.

They asked one person with good character and behavior, "From whom did you learned *hilm*, forbearance?"

He said, "I learned from Qays Ibn al-'Aṣim ق. One day I was sitting in his presence, and a maidservant came to him with a container that had hot charcoal and on it was some hot food. *Wa saqat min yaddiha,* as soon as she came, all this charcoal and the hot container fell down from her hand onto his young son The child died immediately. The servant was afraid, she didn't know what to do. Qays Ibn al-'Aṣim ق said, *la rawa'a 'alayk antī ḥur fillāh,* ' 'Don't be afraid, I am freeing you for Allāh's sake.' She harmed him and he freed her. Although he felt the pain in his heart for his son, he freed her to suppress his ego."

Today, cough suppressants control your cough, but we need tablets to suppress our egos! You can find that in a store that has that medicine: that is *awlīyāullāh*. If you want, they can give you the tablet and in forty days you will be finished from your ego. If they don't give you the tablets they are playing with you, as they know you are not yet ready yet.

Therefore, in order to suppress his ego, Qays Ibn al-'Aṣim freed her, because his ego was saying, "She killed your boy, so kill her." From that pious actions, that person learned forbearance from Qays ibn al-'Asim. It is not easy. If someone kills your child, will you say, "No problem." If you killed someone's child, they will sue you for millions! There was insurance at that time also, heavenly insurance. You will get it in Paradise or in your grave, or you might even get it in *dunyā.*

Stories of Ibrahim ibn al-Adham

Ibrāhīm ibn al-Adham was a king. He is buried in Damascus. Every night, he drank (alcohol) until he fell down. All of his engines would be down, he would vomit and get sick. One night he was sitting in his house looking at the stars through a big glass dome he had built, when he heard someone walking on that dome. He looked and saw a man. Who can come to Ibrāhīm ibn al-Adham, the famous king?

He asked, "What are you doing?"

The man replied, "I am searching for my camel."

"How are you are searching for your camel on my dome?"

We look at others' mistakes and forget our own. He was looking at that one's mistake, but not at his own. We are dipped in our ego's arrogance. Struggle against it, and then Allāh will take you from the Shore of Ignorance to the Shore of Knowledge by *rīḥ aṣ-ṣibā*, the Heavenly Breeze. That is like a tornado, but you will sense the beautiful perfume in it and it will take you to the other shore in the blink of an eye! You don't need more than that. But you need to show continuity, that you are doing your work, your *awrād*, your *dawah,* and what is asked of you by your shaykh. Ibrāhīm ibn al-Adham asked the man what he was doing and not looking at himself that he is drunk.

He said, "How can your camel be here on the third floor, on top of the dome?"

The man said, "There is a possibility to find my camel on your dome, but there is no possibility for you to find your Lord in your current state."

That was like an arrow shot through Ibrāhīm's heart! The people asked him, *hal farihta min ad-dunyā, yā Ibrāhīm,* "Did you enjoy your worldly life, Ibrāhīm?"

He said, "Yes, twice." These are examples that show us the good manners that *awlīyā* carry. He said, "One time I was sitting, *qaʿidan*."

This is part of the story that Grandshaykh ق mentioned about Ibrāhīm ibn al-Adham ق, why he was sitting at that time; because he went to a mosque, as he was going in the way of Allāh. He was cold and bleeding. He entered the mosque, prayed ʿIsha, and lay down. The keeper of the *masjid* kicked him out.

Ibrāhīm ibn al-Adham ق said, "Leave me alone. I am an old man." The servant said, "Even if you were Ibrāhīm ibn al-Adham, I would still throw you out! You are lying!" and he beat Ibrāhīm ibn al-Adham, who left and went under a tree that had a tree house with three people inside. He explained to those who asked about his *dunyā,* "I was sitting there and one of them was drinking. He came out of the tree house and urinated on me. I was so happy and pleased, as he showed me what I deserved. That was one of the happiest things that happened to me in *dunyā,* because *that is dunyā*: to take poison out of the body. I understood it that He is giving me a signal to take out all the poison from my body."

Ibrāhīm continued, "The second time, I was sitting among a group of people and one of them came and slapped me on the face. When he slapped me, *ja'a āḥadahum wa ṣafaʿnī,* he woke me up to the remembrance of the Day of Judgment. Allāh ﷻ might send angels to slap me with no end. He made me aware of what might happen to me, both in the grave and on the Day of Judgment. These were the two times I was so happy from *dunyā,* because these incidents made me realize what *dunyā* is and what is represents."

Look at how much good character he has! One urinated on him and still he said, "No problem." The second one beat him up and he said, "No problem." If someone urinates on us, what will we do? If a baby in diapers urinates on you, you beat them!

It is said, once Ibrāhīm ibn al-Adham ق roamed a jungle in Allāh's love. A soldier passed by and asked, *ayna al-ʿimāra,* "Where is the city?" *ʿAmār* is where you build homes.

Ibrāhīm said, "There is the city."

The soldier took his stick and beat him on the head. He showed the soldier the city, so why did he beat him up? Because he showed him the cemetery, saying, "That is the city you are going to be sleeping in one day." The soldier thought Ibrāhīm was mocking him. He beat him severely, wounding his head.

When the soldier passed by the city, people asked him, "What have you done today?! You beat the most ascetic person in all Khorasan!"

Persia today is one of the main city of *awlīyā;* that is why it is going to be safe, and Mawlana Shaykh Nazim said no one can touch it.

The soldier came back to apologize. Ibrāhīm ibn al-Adham ق said, "When you beat me up, I asked Paradise for you from Allāh!" When someone beats you up, what do you do? Ask for Paradise by going to the police. You don't ask Paradise for him, but instead jail.

The soldier asked, "Why did you do that?"

He said, "Because you brought a reward for me when you beat me up. I didn't want that to be for me only, so I asked Paradise for you. And on the Day of Judgment, I didn't want you to be judged on my account, or to be the cause of your punishment, and I didn't want to be rewarded because you beat me. So I asked Allāh to give you Paradise."

Tolerate Everything that Will Not Take You to Hellfire

Do you ask for Paradise for those who beat you? Look at how they teach children today, they teach them marital arts, to defend themselves. You don't need martial arts. When you surrender to Allāh's will, that is the real martial arts. Ibrāhīm ibn al-Adham ق was able to blow him far away with just one breath, but he didn't. Today they teach young children how to fight the enemy. Your enemy is Shayṭān! Be peaceful and there will be no fight.

It was said by Ḥātim al-Aṣam ق, *ḥusn al-khuluq an yaḥtamil kull wāḥid,* "The best character is to carry whatever they show to you, tolerate and accept them, except for one. Tolerate all else and you will be rewarded, but don't tolerate the one that will take you to Hellfire."

They asked, "Who is that?"

He replied, "That is your ego. Tolerate others for Allāh's sake, but beat your ego by not giving it what it likes."

Malik ibn Dinar ق was a famous *walī,* official, and judge. One lady came to him and said, *yā mura'ī,* "O hypocrite! The one who thinks he is something! He is nothing, and garbage in my eyes!" A lady said this to a big judge, and they say ladies have no rights (in Islam)!

He looked at her, not seeing a man or woman, and replied. "May Allāh bless you. I was looking for the name I lost. Today you came and gave it to me. *Wajadtu 'ismī al-ladhī adAllāhu ahlu 'l-basra,* I found the name that the people of Basra lost. *Alḥamdulillāh,* I am thankful to you."

He didn't tell his army or police to throw her in prison. So what is your name, *mura'ī.* Our name is to "show off" only; we are not dressing in the real dress as there is hypocrisy.

Sayyīdinā Luqmān ﷺ advised his sons to have three characters: *Thalātha la tu'raf illa 'inda thalāth. al-ḥilm 'indal-ghaḍab,* "Three things are only known through three others."

First is, to be patient when getting angry. All these emails that come to us are full of anger. "My wife did that, my neighbor did that." Every day there are hundreds of emails filled with complaints!

Prophet ﷺ said:

Man 'arafa nafsahu faqad 'arafa Rabbahu.
He who knows his self knows his Lord.

We interpret this *ḥadīth* as, "Who knows his bad characters knows his Lord." But *awlīyā* interpret it differently: "Who knows himself, what Allāh is showering on him of Beautiful Names and Attributes, to see the lights that Allāh is showering on us, that one knows his Lord."

Allāh doesn't look at the bad characters, but looks at the lights and manifestations of Allāh's Names. You cannot go to the Divine Presence without these lights as they are the code and password. That is why it is recommended on *Jumu'ah* to take a shower, *ghusl,* as it will clean you, to take you to these manifestations of Divine Lights, and to divine prayer in the Presence of Allāh. Surrender to Allāh's will, don't show anger and complain! Sayyīdinā Luqmān ﷺ is telling his sons to have forbearance, as Prophet ﷺ said to Sayyīdinā Abū Bakr ؓ, *al-ghaḍabū kufrun,* "Anger is unbelief."

Second is, to have courage in war. Are we in war today? Yes, we are in the war against our ego. Not the war where they are blowing innocent people up, saying, "I am going to Paradise." You are going to Hellfire! So are we declaring war against our ego?

The third good character is, to give charity when you know someone is in need. That means to be generous with people and to help them. If someone is sick, help him; if someone is sad, smile at him. Prophet ﷺ said, "A smile is *ṣadaqah.*" To visit a patient or to build a school, all of this is *ṣadaqah. Ṣadaqah* is when someone is in need, you help. That person will find you there. These are the three characters Sayyīdinā Luqmān ﷺ advised his sons to keep.

One *walī* had a servant helping him. People asked, "Why are you keeping him? Set him free."

He said, "I can't set him free because I am learning forbearance from him. He does everything wrong. I am keeping him to learn patience."

One *murīd* invited his shaykh, 'Uthmān al-Hīlī ق, to his house. When he entered through the door, the *murīd* said, "I called you, but now I cannot accommodate you, so please go back." He is a *walī* and shaykh, coming to the house of his *murīd.* This means when the shaykh comes with a stick, don't send him back as he comes with a stick against your ego.

Grandshaykh ق said, "*Awlīyā* look at their *murīds* at least three times a day, and they don't send candies, they send pain, to see how the *murīd* will react."

The *murīd* said, "I regret I called you to my house, you can go now," and the shaykh left.

A few days later, that *murīd* returned to the shaykh and said, "I regret I kicked you out. Please come back." The ego was telling him to fix that. So the shaykh went back. He didn't say, "I am not coming, you threw me one time, that is it," and he would never go. The shaykh went and at the door the host said, "No, sorry again, but I cannot accommodate you. Please go back." And the shaykh went back. The *murīd* did this to him four or five times and finally said to the shaykh, "I did that to try you."

SubhānAllāh fa lillāh ḍarruk! That is a highly respected saying which means, "'Only Allāh knows how high you are,' (that I threw you out four or five times and you never said anything)."

The *murīd* asked, "What kind of *walī* are you and what kind of *khuluq* do you have? You kept on coming, not complaining. I called you back and you kept coming, then I kicked you out. What kind of high character you have? I don't understand!"

The shaykh said, *lā tamdaḥnī fī khuluqin tujid fī 'l-ḥaywān,* "Don't praise me, my son, for a character found in animals."

The *murīd* asked, "O *Sayyīdī*! What is that character that when you call, it will come, and when you kick it out, it goes?"

He said, "That is a dog's character. Don't praise me for that."

This is the first level in *ṭarīqah,* not to say a dog is better, but to learn that there are signs in everything around us. Nothing will stop a lion or a tiger in a jungle, but the goat is different, it eats anything. Or a donkey, which is patient; it carries any amount of load, no matter how heavy. So we have to learn from the characters of what Allāh created for the benefit of *Ummat an-Nabī,* not to be wild. "Don't praise me, because if the dog is invited, it will come, and if thrown, it will go."

It is said that one day that shaykh was passing by a house and someone threw ashes that came all over him, like ashes from a volcano. His *murīds* got upset and began to curse, "That is our shaykh! How dare you throw ashes!" The ones who threw it didn't know, they just threw it from their window. It was not like today, you will get a ticket for "littering."

The shaykh said to them, "Don't get angry. If the one who deserves Hellfire gets a substitute of ashes, he will take the ashes! I was feeling the Hellfire and was saved by ashes thrown on me."

These are examples of good character of *awlīyāullāh.* May Allāh guide us and teach us by means of these stories.

Wa min Allāhi 't-tawfiq, bi ḥurmati 'l-ḥabīb, bi ḥurmati 'l-Fātiḥah.
And with Allāh is success. For the sake of the Beloved, for his sake we recite the opening chapter of Holy Qur'an.

To Be Rightly Guided, Connect to Your True Fathers

A'ūdhu billāhi min ash-Shayṭān ir-rajīm. Bismillāhi' r-Raḥmāni 'r-Raḥīm. Nawaytu 'l-arbā'īn, nawaytu 'l-'itikāf, nawaytu'l-khalwah, nawaytu 'l-'uzlah, nawaytu 'r-riyāḍa, nawaytu 's-sulūk, lillāhi Ta'alā fī hādhā 'l-masjid. Ati' ūllāh wa ati'ū 'r-Rasūl wa ūli 'l-amri minkum. (4:59)

All of us must take examples from what is around us, of which there are many evidences that can give us signs of Allāh's Greatness. If you look at today's technology, you see just now on the Internet they say these programmers have programmed. Allāh gave them ability and logic, and the ability to put programs for people to express themselves. And these programs are based on a specific knowledge they studied, after which they made it possible for people to speak with each other and express themselves. This is what we see on the Internet; programmers put on the Internet a chat for people to say what is in their hearts.

Now, they might say on the Internet all kinds of good things, if they are on the way of Allāh ﷻ, which means they express themselves through sharing their love and inner beliefs with others. What do you think about the one who is in *Sulṭān al-Awlīyā*'s associations? Their chat will be from east to west, not only the chat of *murīds,* but chats of *jinn* and *ins*. And what do you think about chatting on a heavenly Internet about the message of Prophet ﷺ? There will be an infinite number of angels and human beings, century after century, speaking of the greatness of the Prophet ﷺ!

O human beings! Allāh gave us a way to speak to the Prophet ﷺ, a program, to make *munajāt,* to seek his forgiveness through a heavenly chat, but on one condition: to follow that program. The program is set and every *walī* has his own program, and *Sulṭān al-Awlīyā* has combined all these programs reaching to Prophet ﷺ, who has his own program. That is why it is said, *ad-dunyā jīfatun wa ṭulābuhā kilābuhā,* "The *dunyā* is a carcass and those who seek it are wild animals." So that means, follow the program and don't follow *dunyā. Dunyā* will throw us in the Hellfire, and Allāh wants us to be saved through His program. As much as you are strong, as much more programs will open for you. As much as programs are opened, as much as strongly classified spiritual information is given to your heart. *Fa 'alaykum bi ittib'a an-nabī*, "Our duty is to follow the Prophet, *wa kāna khuluqahu al-qur'an*, his character, his manners, were the Holy Qur'an." It means not one verse, not one *sūrah*, but the whole Qur'an! He is *al-Qur'an al-nātiq*, "the talking Qur'an."

Allāh gave the Prophet ﷺ the secret of the Holy Qur'an and from him these secrets, as mentioned in the previous session, *ma ya'lamu ta'wīlahu illa-Allāh war-rāsikhūna fil-'ilm*, no one knows its interpretation except Allāh and those well established in knowledge; they know and say, *amāna*, "We believe." So our duty is to believe and not to question those *awlīyā* that Allāh gave the ability to interpret knowledge; our duty to listen and follow.

Sami'nā wa ata'na ghufrānaka rabbanā wa 'ilayk al-masīr.
We hear and we obey. (We seek) Your forgiveness, our Lord, and to You is the return (of all, so forgive us.) (Sūrat al-Baqarah, 2:285)

If we disobey our *shuyūkh*, that will throw us away. So our duty is to learn to be of the best of character and Prophet ﷺ is the best of characters, and his *awlīyā* whom Allāh granted to carry the flag of Prophet until Judgment Day, until when Sayyīdinā Mahdī ؑ appears and *awlīyā* deliver their flags to Sayyīdinā Mahdī ؑ. Then there are no more flags at that time except his flag, which is the secret of the Holy Qur'an!

I heard Grandshaykh ق say, in the time of Mahdī ؑ, if you open a printed Qur'an of today you will not see any writings as it is printed with *dunyā* ink, and a heavenly Qur'an will come revealed in heavenly printing, and lights will come from every letter. When you look at the Holy Qur'an that was delivered to *Ṣaḥābah* ؓ, it is full with light, and the *Ṣaḥābah* were able to take from the lights of every letter, and it was opened for *awlīyāullāh*. Sayyīdinā Mahdī ؑ is waiting to come with those secrets! So our duty is to find our relationship and get the best characteristics, and to do that is to follow your teacher, as they are our spiritual fathers.

Allāh ﷻ said:

Ad'ūhum li-ābā'ihim Hūwa aqsaṭu.
Call them to their fathers; that is more just with Allāh.
(Sūrat al-'Aḥzāb, 33:5)

Ad'ūhum li-ābā'ihim, from the father to the mother, and then a child comes. So, "Call them to their fathers, to be known who is the father." It can be any father, you don't know. So a child has be named his father's name and even in western countries they put the wife's name following the husband's, and then her family name becomes like the husband's. You have to know your fathers all the way to Prophet ﷺ. If you don't know, you make a mistake. Allāh will forgive you, but try.

Sayyīdinā ʿAbdu 'l-Wahhāb ash-Shaʿrānī ق, one of the big scholars and big saints of Islam, said, *man lā yaʿlamu abā'uhu wa ajdādud fa huw aʿam*, "Who doesn't know his father and grandfather in *ṭarīqah* is blind, like someone who doesn't see at all." And it might be by mistake he will go to another father, as he is blind and doesn't know, so he doesn't connect to his true father. You cannot connect to another one, as the Prophet said:

laʿnAllāhu man antasaba ila ghayra abīh.
Who connects to whom is not his real father will be cursed.

If you connect to another shaykh, it means you are not trying to research the real connection; then you will be cursed as one who connects to whom is not his real father. So in our creation, the soul is more connected to your reality, and Allāh ﷻ created the soul first. *Al-arwāhu junūdan mujanada*, "Souls are like battalion in groups." Allāh called all these souls on the Day of Promises and asked, "Am I not your Lord?" They replied, "Yes!"

Wa idh ākhadha rabbuka min banī ādama min ẓuhūrihim dhurriyyatahum wa ashhadahum ʿalā anfusihim alastu bi-rabbikum qalū balā shahidnā an taqūlu yawma 'l-qīyāmati innā kunnā ʿan hadha ghāfilīn.
When your Lord drew forth from the loins Children of Adam their descendants, and made them testify concerning themselves, (saying), "Am I not your Lord (Who cherishes and sustains you)?" They said, "Yes! We do testify!" (This), unless you will say on the Day of Judgment, "Of this we were never mindful." (Sūrat al-Aʿrāf, 7:172)

"Am I not your Lord?" They said, "Yes." Who was there? Our realities, connected with the soul there and we knew we were Allāh's servants there, we accepted. Can you say no when you are seeing the Truth? Those are good tidings that everyone was in the Divine Presence. So the soul was created first then the body.

That is why Prophet ﷺ said, "I was a prophet when Adam was *bayni 'r-rūḥi wa 'l-jasad*, between soul and body. I was a Prophet already in *ruh* and Adam was still between *ruh* and body."

And from And from 'Abd ar-Razzāq's *Mūṣannaf*, we take the *ḥadīth* of Prophet ﷺ, "The first thing that Allāh created is my Light."

The Spiritual Father and the Biological Father

So we take the soul first and then *jasad*, body, as you take the spiritual father first and then the biological father. Good tidings to the one whose biological father is the same as his spiritual father! In the previous times, for a long time they taught the students and followers, *adab abā'ihim*, the best manners of their parents and to know *ansābihim*, their lineage. That is for the physical connection, so what do you think about the spiritual connection with the father of your soul?

It is said that Sayyīdinā Abū Bakr aṣ-Ṣiddīq ق is the spiritual father of all Naqshbandi followers. The one who doesn't know or who didn't find his spiritual father has no right to sit and teach! His teaching is disconnected unless he will humble himself and find his spiritual father, going back to Prophet ﷺ. *Alḥamdulillāh*, we are connected with *as-Silsilat adh-Dhabiyya*, the Golden Chain!

Many authors of spirituality have mentioned that is a golden chain, as it connects through Sayyīdinā Abū Bakr ؓ on one side and through Sayyīdinā 'Alī ؓ on the other side, through Sayyīdinā Jafar aṣ-Ṣadiq ق. Those who have been authorized to give lectures, who have guidance from their fathers all the way to Prophet ﷺ, there is light in their speeches. We are so lucky!

Grandshaykh, may Allāh bless his soul, I quote him and people might say, "Why do you quote him so much and not Mawlana Shaykh Nazim?" There is no reason, except people hear from many sources about Mawlana Shaykh Nazim, but few are hearing from Grandshaykh. So we quote from that, in order to have a taste of what our grandfather taught, and from him we learn a lot about his spiritual father, Shaykh Sharafuddīn ق and his lineage to Prophet ﷺ.

Grandshaykh ق said, "What is the wisdom of going to the Cave Thawr when going from Mecca to Madinah? Was not Prophet ﷺ able to go to Madinah without passing through that cave? He was able to do so."

We have mentioned it before, but when watching a video on your computer and it "buffers" you press "F5". Why F5, and not F4? I don't know. Why not F6? What does F5 mean and what does F6 mean? I don't know, but they press F5 and it refreshes the connection. To refresh our memory we press F5, and all the pictures come back. That means in every heart there is an F5 button, and if we press it, brings everything back.

As for Allāh ﷻ, there is no past and no future! Always there is that moment you are in, here, and in the grave, and in Paradise. Don't look at the moment that is coming; the *adab* is to always reflect, "Am I good now, or not?" Fix yourself.

So press F5 and then in a moment everything comes. That is why when *awlīyā* mention a story from the past, they are living it as if they are in it, hearing and seeing and being there; to them that is F5. So he was relating that story and it was as if he was living that story, and for you it becomes like a living scene and you are in it, because *awlīyāullāh* don't tell you a story with no wisdom. No, you must enter it and you feel you are there.

One time I was *bayḍ ṣuḥafu*, transcribing from raw notes of *ṣuḥbat* and rewriting in a notebook. I share this with you, never mind, and suddenly I came across *baya*ʿ and as I came across that I felt myself not writing anymore but the whole scenery changed, and I saw Grandshaykh, may Allāh bless his soul, and Mawlana Shaykh standing there. Grandshaykh said, "Extend your hand." At that moment, I went to extend my hand and I saw Prophet's hand come in and then 124,000 prophets' hands came and Prophet's hand was on top, then Grandshaykh's hand and then 124,000 saints' hands.

Grandshaykh said, "Put your hand," and then I felt Allāh's ﷻ Hands come on top and then I heard recitation of *Āyat al-Baya*ʿ. I was in that kind of vision or whatever you want to call it, a living scene. So these things happen. *Awlīyāullāh* can push a button and bring everything, and it is not difficult for them.

So when he was mentioning about the migration of Prophet ﷺ to Madinatu 'l-Munawwara, he said the wisdom of passing through Ghāri Thawr is to transfer the secrets from Prophet's heart to Sayyīdinā Abū Bakr aṣ-Ṣiddīq's heart, and to put *Kalīmat at-Tawḥīd*, which is *dhikr* of *lā ilāha illa-Llāh*, and also to put the recitation of *ʿIsm adh-Dhāt*, "Allāh," on the tongues of the spiritual children of Abū Bakr aṣ-Ṣiddīq!

Qul Allāh thumma dharhum fī khawdihim yalʿabūn.
Say, "Allāh," then leave them to play in their vain discussions.

(Sūrat al-'Anʿām, 6:91)

So he ordered Sayyīdinā 'Abdul Khāliq al-Ghujdawāni ق and it was put on the tongue of Sayyīdinā 'Abdul Khāliq, *Allāhu, Allāhu, Allāhu Ḥaqq. Allāhu, Allāhu, Allāhu Ḥaqq. Allāhu, Allāhu, Allāhu Ḥaqq.* And Sayyīdinā 'Abdul Khāliq was ordered to call all Naqshbandi *murīds* coming in the future to be the spiritual children of Abū Bakr aṣ-Ṣiddīq.

They were called to the presence of Prophet ﷺ to Ghāri Thawr, where they all appeared. Not only that, but anyone who comes to ask you a question during the *dhikr* will be among them, as they are those who, *lā yashqa jalīsahum,* "Will never see a bad end in his life." He said, "All of them," and that means us also, migrated with Sayyīdinā Muḥammad ﷺ from Mecca to Madinah in the spiritual dimension, and will be given the reward of immigrants from *dunyā* to *Ākhirah*!

When he was speaking about that scene, it was as if they were living it; for them it was not a story. If our hearts were strong we felt every moment of that story, we had goose bumps! So it is a live scene, not like watching a movie. The actors in the movie are living the story, and you are watching, but in the Naqshbandi Order we press our "F5" refresh button to live the story, so that past becomes present.

Wa wada' al-mīzān allā tatghaw fi 'l-mīzān. Wa aqim al-waznu bil-qisṭi wa lā tukhsiru 'l-mīzān.
And He has set up the Balance, that you may not transgress (due) balance, but observe the measure with equity and do not fall short of it.
(Sūrat ar-Raḥmān, 55:7-9)

So establish the weight justly, don't transgress in the balance. Don't make one side heavier than the another, except for *ḥasanāt*. Are you going to refresh your F5? *Inshā'Allāh.*

May Allāh ﷻ forgive us and may Allāh ﷻ bless us.

Wa min Allāhi 't-tawfiq, bi ḥurmati 'l-ḥabīb, bi ḥurmati 'l-Fātiḥah.
And with Allāh is success. For the sake of the Beloved, for his sake we recite the opening chapter of Holy Qur'an.

The Secrets of Talqin

A'ūdhu billāhi min ash-Shayṭān ir-rajīm. Bismillāhi' r-Raḥmāni 'r-Raḥīm. Nawaytu 'l-arbā'īn, nawaytu 'l-'itikāf, nawaytu'l-khalwah, nawaytu 'l-'uzlah, nawaytu 'r-riyāḍa, nawaytu 's-sulūk, lillāhi Ta'alā fī hādhā 'l-masjid. Ati' ūllāh wa ati'ū 'r-Rasūl wa ūli 'l-amri minkum. (4:59)

Everyone must know their relationships, especially with their father. And you have to search well in order to reach a perfect teacher and perfect guide connected to Prophet ﷺ through a lineage of *awlīyāullāh* that take you there. That is why what you receive depends upon the level of that *silsilah,* chain. If that *silsilah* of *awlīyāullāh* that goes to Prophet ﷺ is a Golden Chain, then you are lucky. If the chain is lower than that, then you are still lucky, and even if is at the first level, still you are lucky. However, what you take depends on the strength of that chain.

That is why Muḥammad al-Busayrī ق knew the secret of that through his heart, which was always connected to the heart of Prophet, and he dropped *dunyā* completely from his heart. If we don't drop *dunyā* there will still be obstacles and veils. And Muḥammad al-Busayrī, who is connected to the heart of Prophet ﷺ, said in his famous verse of poetry, *wa kullun min rasūlullāhi multamisan,* "Everyone is seeking and trying to get something, requesting, sending a petition, 'Please, *yā Rasūlullāh,* give us something!'"

And when he says, *kullun min Rasūlullāhi multamisan, "kullun"* doesn't mean only you and me, or that one and that one, but it means everyone: every prophet, every *Ṣaḥābī,* and every creature Allāh created, and not only *dunyā* creatures, but *Ākhirah* heavenly creatures, as well! And that means everyone and everything to whom Allāh gave life is moving with that life, and they are in need of a connection with Prophet ﷺ, which means anything that is moving, not one will be left out.

Even the Earth is moving and it needs to turn from Prophet ﷺ! Allāh ﷻ created Creation and raised the Prophet to a very high station, *qāba qawsayni aw adnā,* "Two bows length or nearer." Everyone must to acknowledge respect of Prophet ﷺ because, as we know, Allāh raised the name of Prophet and put it with His Name! A name without an appearance is not enough, so when that appearance appeared, it had a name, and that is why they appear, because of Prophet ﷺ!

What are they saying about the *ḥadīth* of Jabir ؓ in the *Muṣānnaf* of ʿAbdu 'r-Razzāq, although they say it is not mentioned or not found or not true, that is the limit of their *ʿilm* they did not reach. But in the understanding of *awlīyā,* they ask Prophet ﷺ directly for anything they need, or else what is the benefit of being *awlīyā,* if they are not able to reach and ask the Prophet ﷺ?

Everyone accepts that Allāh ﷻ raised Prophet's name with His Name, and that to raise the name without the appearance is nothing. The missing part (in their understanding) is, you must have the appearance that is living. So when Prophet ﷺ said, "The first thing Allāh created was my light," then Allāh created that appearance of Muḥammad and raised him to His Presence. And that is the missing part that *awlīyā* are exposing. I cannot say, "Your name is ʿAli," if you are not appearing; how can I give you a name? The name signifies the reality. So the name of Prophet that has been raised to *lā ilāha illa-Llāh Muḥammadun Rasūlullāh* means the name signifies that he is there.

That is missing in the *ḥadīth* of Prophet ﷺ that all scholars accept:

Kuntu nabīyyin wa adamu bayna 'l-mā'i wa 't-tīn.

I was a prophet when Adam was between water and clay.

And two other *riwayats* are accepted, meaning that Sayyīdinā Muḥammad ﷺ was a prophet before Adam ؑ, and Allāh raised his name, which means He raised the significance of "Muḥammad," where He created his Light before all Creation, or else how will he be a symbol of all Creation? He is the one who Allāh will speak to and that is the reality that Muḥammad al-Busayrī ؓ knew. He said, *wa kullun min rasūlullāhi multamisan,* "Everyone is in need of Prophet to reach them." That means Prophet's Light was created before anything else, in order that, *mustamidūn min nur an-nabī,* "everything in movement receives support from the Light of Prophet." Everyone is taking from the heart of Prophet ﷺ!

And Muḥammad al-Busayrī ؓ said, *gharfan min al-baḥr aw rashfan min ad-diyami,* "Taking a huge amount of water from the ocean of Prophet, in huge containers (*gharfan*)," and *rashfan,* "sipping." So even at that lower level, you are taking from Prophet ﷺ through *awlīyā,* who take you and up, up, up, to reach to the reality of that Golden Chain. And we ask Allāh to keep us with the Golden Chain that takes from both Sayyīdinā Abū Bakr ☙ and Sayyīdinā 'Alī ☙! So if you take from *shaykh al-kāmil*, a perfect master, a high-level guide that is known from that Order, that he dressed in the *khirqah*, cloak, and his shaykh dressed from his shaykh's cloak, all the way to Prophet ﷺ, it means that pipe open to your heart is a pipe of guidance.

And you must understand that a guide of *irshād* is completely different from a guide doing *dhikrūllāh*. There are many *muqaddims*; Mawlana Shaykh, may Allāh give him long life, said there might be hundreds, but not all are guides. The one who is a guide dresses in the *khirqah* that has a connection to Sayyīdinā Muḥammad ﷺ. That guide is given the permission and authority to guide and make *talqīn*, to put *dhikr* on your heart. An example of that authority is like on computers or TVs, when you press the "menu" button and there is a big list of options: installing, settings, tools, colors, and you check one-after-one.

Talqīn is from the shaykh being given authority from his shaykh, and from his shaykh up to Prophet ﷺ, to guide you, and his authority includes a menu. Some guides are given a menu for *dhikr*, they cannot go more, like some TVs have a limited menu, and others have a sophisticated, higher-level menu with many different functions. So the one who is authorized to put the secret of *talqīn* on tongues and hearts takes his menu from his shaykh, all the way to Prophet ﷺ. And whenever the *murīd* is in need, the shaykh presses that menu button and chooses what he needs for that *murīd*. The secret of *talqīn* is that menu which connects you to the heart of Prophet!

As today, in technology they say, "We need a network to reach everyone," and they have these servers that process millions of emails, and from there they can reach everyone through email. So *awlīyā* have that server to reach everyone who has a connection. So you have to know, the secret of the menu that the shaykh put in heart of *murīds* is networking. So just now our cameraman was late for the live broadcast, and what did they do? One person sent a direct "tweet" (on Twitter.com) from here and informed many people, "The live broadcast is delayed because our cameraman is sleeping."

In similitude, the cameraman is the one who can see the hearts of people. There is a cameraman for *awlīyā*. They are the ones who can reach the hearts of people and see what is there. So in one moment, if you become heedless, that connection is interrupted; it "buffers" and the connection is gone. So then people will say, "What happened? We can no longer see." Of course! You have to be careful from whom you are taking your knowledge, and that cameraman must always be present.

Awliya Are Always Present and Always Inheriting

Awlīyā are always present, not like the *dunyā* cameraman; they are always ready to give you what you need from Prophet ﷺ, that secret to connect the heart of the *murīd* with the shaykh, to Prophet ﷺ, and to the Divine Presence.

Whoever takes initiation (*baya'*), that menu and secret is put on the tongue and heart. Some might have fewer functions, like volume and color, and some might have more and higher functions as in a plasma TV with many different programs and even connection to the Internet. So if that *murīd* reached the level of *talqīn,* if he opens his mouth to talk or his heart to send to the hearts of others, *idhā ḥaraka as-silsilah,* if he moved in his menu to advise, the whole *silsilah* will begin to move to reach that person! That is for one; all who he reaches are ordered to move immediately, *tujawib arwāḥ al-awlīyā,* and if he only shakes his menu it will open to all.

The grandshaykh of that *ṭarīqah* will be moving to reach him, and all the souls of *awlīyā* will be moving to reach that person, and Prophet ﷺ will move immediately to bring that one, with authority to give *talqīn* on his tongue, to reach the Divine Presence, *al-ḥadarat al-ilāhī.* So all that chain will move, from that shaykh to all the shaykhs, to Prophet, to the Divine Presence.

That is why Mawlana Shaykh Nazim always says, "These knowledges are sent to me. I come empty and what they send, I speak." And I am surprised, it is now more than two years, every day, every day, and before also when we used to sit in the 60's and 70's, every day he speaks. It is not easy, not like a professor who sits to prepare notes, not like *dunyā* knowledge. Here, in these associations, there is no subject. Here there is a menu! They have heavenly servers and email and when they connect, it comes immediately.

Today some students decide to research Naqshbandi Ṭarīqah for their PhD thesis. They check the biography of every grandshaykh of the Golden Chain, but that *silsilah* will not move as they don't have the menu, not even if they mention their names, because they are "outsiders," and only "insiders" have the menu. Any one of Mawlana's *murīds,* according to the menu he has been given, can activate and move the *silsilah* by that power given to him, using his password with that menu. That is why *awlīyāullāh* have been given "the perfect *khilāfah*," *al-khilāfat al-tāmmat al-muṭlaq*. They reach the perfect level; "*al-muṭlaqa*" means their menu has no restriction, it has full authority.

These are grandshaykhs; they are not normal like us. They give something to keep encouragement in the hearts of *murīds* to continue on the Way. That is why they say every *murīd* is a diplomat, as they carry the flag of the shaykh. *Murīd*-to-*murīd* they attract each other, and the *ḥusn al-khuluq*, best characteristics, will attract others to the shaykh, like a hunter has helpers to attract their prey. *Murīds* are always helping the hunter to get his prey by talking to and attracting people. That is why there is *majam'a aṭ-ṭarā'iq*, the compound where all *shuyūkh* of different *ṭarīqahs* meet, like a university campus with many buildings, where many different *ṭuruq* coming to Prophet come together, and don't think they don't come together. Grandshaykh ق gave authority to Mawlana Shaykh Nazim ق on 41 *ṭarīqahs*, not just one. That Golden Chain is one which can overlook all other chains. That is why the Naqshbandi Ṭarīqah is taking from the two doors, Sayyīdinā Abū Bakr ﴿ and Sayyīdinā 'Alī ﴿.

And so all that is in the menu; what is in the hearts of *awlīyā* is to teach you to have *ḥusn al-khuluq* and obedience and modesty, and to carry all these kinds of behaviors. And beyond that, they put on your tongue two levels of *dhikr*: Maqām at-Tawḥīd, which is to deny and confirm, *nafiy wa ithbat*, that is the first step; and, *dhikr* of Allāh's Beautiful Name that encompasses all other Names, "Allāh."

> *Qul Allāh thumma dharhum fī khawdihim yal'abūn.*
> *Say, "Allāh," then leave them to play in their vain discussions.*
> (Sūrat al-'An'ām, 6:91)

It means, "O Prophet! Don't listen to those who are not with you, just as there came to Mūsā light before you! Say "Allāh," and let them play and waste their time!" And that is what we are trying to explain in a symbolic way, that *lā ilāha illa-Llāh* shows us the path. When we reach the end by denying and confirming, deny and confirm more and more, until you deny completely everything from *dunyā* and affirm everything from *Ākhirah*. Then you reach the Divine Presence and you recite *'Ism adh-Dhāt*, "Allāh".

That is what *awlīyāullāh* want their followers to do! *'Ism at-Tawḥīd*, *lā ilāha illa-Llāh*, is a Name that describes all that is possible and which has an appearance. So *dunyā* appearances want you to make *dhikr* of *lā ilāha illa-Llāh,* to deny and cancel appearances you desire through your heart. Recitations of *lā ilāha illa-Llāh* take away these appearances and leaves you clean.

The Process of Denying and Confirming

So by denying and confirming, you are wiping clean all dust of human nature of this life. You are completely wiping all the dust of the appearances of everything in this human life that we are in from the face of the unique *Maqām al-Āḥadīyyah,* the Level of Uniqueness that takes you to Allāh's *'Ism adh-Dhāt* in the Divine Presence, described by the Unique Name of the Essence that encompasses all Names and Attributes. So by denying human desires, you will confirm all these lights that the Divine Presence is carrying. That is why *awlīyā* say there are not only Ninety-nine Names, but the Absolute Unknown Reality of the Creator, Allāh's Divine Essence. They say even the Prophet ﷺ cannot know anything about the Divine Essence except what appears from these Beautiful Name and Attributes, an infinite number of which that can be taken from the heart of Prophet ﷺ!

When you deny the human life, slowly the dust that covers your heart begins to clear up, until it becomes a transparent vision, until you reach the divine fountain. That is *mā'rifatullāh,* not by *Dhāt,* the Essence, but to know Allāh by His Beautiful Names and Attributes that is given to Prophet and now given to *awlīyā.*

Before you had TV that doesn't show except a fuzzy picture, not clear, in black and white; then came color TV, then came high-definition TV, and then plasma TV. So by that path of denial and confirmation and then reaching the Level of Uniqueness, it means you see everything in *dunyā* indicating a Creator. *Maqām al-Āḥadīyyah* is the "Level of Uniqueness" and at that level you can visualize things with a high-definition screen. Still you are looking on the screen, but when you go further you will be living what is on the screen as if it is part of your life. You will have three dimensions as they have today 3D movies and TV. You will see things moving up as if you are in that scene.

So *awlīyā* take their followers to *Maqām at-Talqīn,* by denying and confirming, and then to *Maqām 'Ism adh-Dhāt* and *Maqām al-Āḥadīyyah,* where you see the beauty coming from the Divine Presence and you will be dressed in that. As you continue, you will have *dawām al-ḥuḍūr,* "continuity of presence," which doesn't come until you love that presence.

That is why the first level is *maḥabatūllāh, maḥabbat al-ḥabīb, maḥabbat ash-shaykh.* You have that love as shown by gathering in the presence of the shaykh; if there is no love, you don't come. When you have that love then always you will be present; you have *ḥuḍūr.* In that state, you never forget you are a servant to Allāh; you always remember His Name through *dhikrūllāh* on the tongue and heart. So *dawām a-ḥuḍūr* is a miracle of *awlīyā.*

It is not a miracle to walk on water or fly in air or walk on coal or put knives in your body, no. *Karamāt* al-Awlīyā is *dawām at-tawfiq,* continuity of being present with Allāh and with His Prophet. That will lead to *Maqām al-Āḥadīyyah,* and we will discuss that next time. We thank our cameramen that came at the end. If the cameraman is not here that *ṣuḥbah* will not be taped, but even if he is not here and it is not taped physically, that *ṣuḥbah* will be taped on our hearts. When we have transparency we will be able to download that from our connection to our *mashaykh,* and that is coming to *Sulṭān al-Awlīyā* through his connection, and whatever he gets he is downloading to us. And may Allāh give us long life to see Sayyīdinā Mahdī عليه السلام!

The importance is the missing link between *nūr an-Nabī,* to be created first when Allāh raised the name with His Name; there must be something there to get that appearance and name. And at the door of the Divine Presence no one can enter as written there is, *lā ilāha illa-Llāh,* which means Allāh ﷻ is saying, "I was a Hidden Treasure," and when Creation was created, you deny *dunyā* and all that is other than Allāh and confirm by looking only to that Hidden Treasure, which is still hidden.

May Allāh ﷻ forgive us and may Allāh ﷻ bless us.

Wa min Allāhi 't-tawfiq, bi ḥurmati 'l-ḥabīb, bi ḥurmati 'l-Fātiḥah.
And with Allāh is success. For the sake of the Beloved, for his sake we recite the opening chapter of Holy Qur'an.

The Divine Dress of Kalimat at-Tawhid

A'ūdhu billāhi min ash-Shayṭān ir-rajīm. Bismillāhi' r-Raḥmāni 'r-Raḥīm. Nawaytu 'l-arbā'īn, nawaytu 'l-'itikāf, nawaytu'l-khalwah, nawaytu 'l-'uzlah, nawaytu 'r-riyāḍa, nawaytu 's-sulūk, lillāhi Ta'alā fī hādhā 'l-masjid. Ati' ūllāh wa ati'ū 'r-Rasūl wa ūli 'l-amri minkum. (4:59)

There is no salvation except with the kings and *sulṭāns* of this life and the Next. *Allāhummā sallī 'alā Sayyīdinā Muḥammad wa 'alā ālihi Sayyīdinā Muḥammad.* With hi-tech capability you can see everywhere from where you are. Also you have to notice that Allāh ﷻ has created angels especially to observe through, if we can say this, their continuous heavenly cameras.

They are observing the *'amal* of Bani Adam. We are always under observation in whatever we do and try to progress. Those who are on the right path and the right track will find at the end what Allāh ﷻ promised them. Those who are one day on the right track, and one day on the wrong track, like us, they are struggling, but with Allāh's ﷻ mercy, one day with His *ināya*t, Divine Care, they will arrive there. And there are those who are never interested in the right track or wrong track, they go on their own way. We cannot judge them because we are not judges, so we leave them and Allāh ﷻ will judge them.

This is a beginning, and I would like to mention that tonight our *Sulṭān al-Awlīyā*, Shaykh Nazim al-Haqqani ق, opened something of hidden knowledge about what is going to be seen in these coming days or weeks or months, or more. This is to give a taste to his students, his followers, and to prepare them through their hearts for major events that might and will take place. We mentioned why we are explaining the importance of preparing a power in ourselves, in order to face these coming, major events, and he reminded us with the verse:

> *Wa a'idda lahum mastaṭā'tum min quwattin wa min ribāṭi 'l-khayl turḥibūn bihi 'adūwullāh wa 'adūwakum, wa ākhirīn la t'alamūnahum, Allāhu ya'lamahum wa mā tunfiqū min shay'in fī sabīlillāh yuwaffa ilaykum wa antum lā tuẓlamūn.*

Against them make ready your strength to the utmost of your power, including steeds of war, to strike terror into (the hearts of) the enemies of Allāh and your enemies, and others whom you may not know but whom Allāh knows. Whatever you shall spend in the cause of Allāh shall be repaid to you, and you shall not be treated unjustly. (Sūrat al-'Anfāl, 8:60)

Wa a'idda lahum mastatātum min quwattin, to prepare whatever possibility of power is necessary, *turhibūn bihi 'adūwuallāh,* through which you frighten Allāh's and your enemy. That preparation means you need a weapon, not what we think of in the physical or *dunyā* meaning, as Allāh doesn't need that. Allāh doesn't need us to carry an M-16 or *dunyā* weapons. But He wants us to prepare a very sharp weapon that destroys the kingdom of Shayṭān, Allāh's enemy, the biggest enemy. Allāh is not an enemy to anyone, Allāh is merciful to everyone, but Iblīs and Shayṭān and his army and followers, *shayatīn,* are enemies to everyone, as Shayṭān disobeyed his Lord.

So the enemy is within ourselves. *Awlīyāullāh* are preparing those on the track, who are one day this way and one day the other way, *thumma āmanū, thumma kafarū,* "Those who believe, then disbelieve." (4:137), to give them a sharp spiritual sword against Shayṭān, and that door of the right track is open for all *awlīyā,* and that has never changed.

Mina al-mu'uminīna rijālun ṣadaqū mā 'ahadūllāha 'alayhi fa-minhum man qaḍā naḥbahu wa minhum man yantaẓiru wa mā baddalū tabdīlā.
Among the believers are men who have been true to their covenant with Allāh; of them some have fulfilled their obligations and some of them are still waiting, but they have never changed in the least (Sūrat al-'Aḥzāb, 33:23)

The Spiritual Door that Opened Now

Rijālun, men who have reached the level of manhood—who always kept on the right track with their covenant to Allāh ﷻ and who never changed—they are preparing *Ummat an-Nabī.* They reached a different level of manhood and are preparing their followers. That door opened in the beginning of Ramadan, and today Mawlana said to mention that we are speaking of knowledge about the importance of *dhikrūllāh* through two levels: *lā ilāha illa-Llāh* and *Allāh. Lā ilāha illa-Llāh* is the sword Allāh ﷻ gave *Ummat an-Nabī* that is sharp enough to cut Shayṭān completely and prepare us for the appearance of Sayyīdinā Mahdī ☝!

Many people are sleeping and do not know anything about Mahdī ☝, while some people know and are not following, and others know and are waiting. You are of the group that knows and is waiting! The time is coming shortly. If you want to believe, you believe. If you don't want to believe, it is up to you. Things don't come suddenly without plans. We plan for ten to twenty years. From pre-Eternal, when there was no Creation, Allāh's Will was already declared to the one that was a prophet when Adam ☝ was still between soul and body! It was declared to him what is Allāh's will, and when Mahdī will appear in the Last Days.

They know, and we don't know as we are veiled; it is going to be surprise! Do we know when a tsunami will come? When it comes it takes everyone. Do we know when an earthquake will come? With all their technology and machines, they never anticipate accurately when there will be an earthquake. Does anyone know when a tornado or hurricane will come? Did they know when the eruption of a volcano in Scotland would be? They (awliyā) don't tell you when you will die in order to keep you on the right track, so they hide, to see if we remain straight-forward or not. It's no problem if you go here and there, to either side of the track, as long as you are on the right track and as long as you are struggling.

There are some, however, who are not interested; they are thumma āmanū, thumma kafarū. I am sorry to say, some don't know where is qiblah (direction Muslims face in prayer, towards Mecca), and they call themselves "activists" for Muslims and for Islam. How are you an activist for Islam and you don't know where is qiblah even in your own home? We say, may Allāh save them and us, and guide them and us!

That power that we were speaking of from the beginning of Ramadan to today, they dressed us not only with the explanation, but as if you entered it, and they dressed you as if you have done it! Like that, we appear in their presence and from there to the presence of Prophet ☝, and he is taking us to the Divine Presence of Allāh ☝! And we only heard about Kalīmat at-Tawḥīd, dhikr of lā ilāha illa-Llāh, but we never manifested anything of that. But our spirit can see and it is dipped in that ocean of Kalīmat at-Tawḥīd, denying and confirming, as if we passed that level to the higher level of the dhikr by 'Ism adh-Dhāt, "Allāh".

Mawlana said to mention that everyone of us has a spiritual sword, "And if their hand is not moving, our hand is moving that, and we are the ones holding and moving their hand against Shayṭān and their ego." And he said, "Say to them they have been dressed with not only that spiritual power, but they have been dressed in any meeting they attend, and anywhere they attended they, and all *murīds* (of Mawlana Shaykh), have been under every session with 70,000 different lights appearing on them, in the presence of the Prophet ﷺ."

In every session there are 70,000 lights, *shawariq al-anwār,* "the ascending lights." And to everyone Allāh gave different lights; all 70,000 lights are unique to each person! And that is a good tiding that Mawlana Shaykh gave on *Laylat al-Jumuʿah,* that he said to mention, as a reward, because that *Laylat al-Qadr* is coming and Ramadan is ending. We will see later what he says for *Laylat al-Qadr, insha'Allāh.*

What we said before, we have to know that the best example of *Kalīmat at-Tawḥīd, lā ilāha illa-Llāh,* is *Miʿrāj.* The first part of *Miʿrāj* was moving in *dunyā;* the 'Isrā' was when Prophet ﷺ moved from Mecca to Jerusalem, from Masjid al-Ḥarām to Masjid al-Aqsa.

> *Subḥāna al-ladhī asrā bi ʿabdihi laylān mina 'l-masjidi 'l-ḥarāmi ilā al-masjidi'l-'aqsā'l-ladhī bāraknā ḥawlahu linūrīyahu min ayātinā innahu Hūwa as-Samīʿu 'l-Baṣīr.*
> *Glory be to Him Who took His servant for a journey by night from Al-Masjid-al-Ḥarām (at Mecca) to the farthest mosque (in Jerusalem), the neighbourhood We have blessed, so We might show him Our ayāt (signs), for verily, He is the All-Hearer, the All-Seeing.* (Sūrat al-Isrāʿ, 17:1)

It means, praise be to Allāh ﷻ that He moved His perfect human being, Sayyīdinā Muḥammad ﷺ, from the *masjid* in which no sin can be committed, Masjid al-Ḥaram (*ḥarām* means "forbidden"); there is no sin there, and if anyone commits a sin there it will be immediately burned by the Divine Light descending there. So whoever enters there is going to be peaceful, in safety and peace. As Grandshaykh ق said, *lā yumkin an yatadanas,* "there, there is no possibility of becoming dirty from people's sin. Sin immediately disappears there, it is burned completely, it disintegrates. Whoever enters in it, finished! He is there, it is what we explained at the beginning, that the heart is also a place in which these lights appear. "Neither My Heaven nor My Earth contain Me, but the heart of the believer contains Me." So in *Maqām al-Qalbi,* "the Level of the Heart," you will be clean as there is no dirtiness there when you enter, but until you enter there is still a grey area. *Kalīmat at-Tawḥīd* takes you from these grey areas to the area of safety, peacefulness, and lights.

The best example of this is in *Isrā'*, when Prophet was moved from Masjid al-Ḥarām where there is no sin, to the Masjid al-Aqsa, Masjid of the Dome in Jerusalem, where he began his *Mi'rāj. Isrā'* is a movement within Creation through recitation of *lā ilāha illa-Llāh,* followed by ascension. Ascension is upward through the universe, going beyond the limits of this *dunyā* with all its universes, which has been created with all its galaxies. Prophet ﷺ moved and was able to reach the heavenly Creation, which is still under *lā ilāha illa-Llāh.*

In that Holy Ascension, Sayyīdinā Jibrīl knocked at the door of every Heaven.

They asked, "Who is with you?"

He replied, "The Seal of Messengers is with me."

"Has he been invited?"

"Yes."

Only after this exchange and answering correctly, the door opens, and it continued like that until after the Seventh Paradise, and Sayyīdinā Jibrīl said to Prophet ﷺ, "*Yā Rasūlullāh*! I cannot go forward, you go!" The Station of *Tawḥīd* ends there. There was no one moving in that reality except Prophet. There is the manifestation of *'Ism adh-Dhāt*, under which comes all the Beautiful Names and Attributes. He entered that station alone, where those are the lights given to the heart of Prophet ﷺ.

Mā wasi'anī arḍī wa lā arḍī wa lākin wasi'anī qalbi 'abdī al-mu'min.
Neither Earth nor Heavens contained Me, but the heart of the believer contained Me.
Wa annahu lamā qāma 'abdAllāh yadū'hu kādū yakūna 'alayhi libada.
Yet when the Servant of Allāh stands forth to invoke Him, they just make round him a dense crowd. (Sūrat al-Jinn, 72:19)

Who is "'AbdAllāh"? The only one mentioned in Qur'an as "'AbdAllāh" is Sayyīdinā Muḥammad ﷺ. When he stood up for His Lord, the people were not happy with that. He is the only one and the right one to carry that name, and no one can carry that name in *Ākhirah* except Sayyīdinā

Muḥammad ﷺ! You can be "'Abdur-Raḥmān," or "'Abdul-Ḥafīẓ," but "'AbdAllāh" is only for Sayyīdinā Muḥammad ﷺ! That is why Turkish people have such real belief in Prophet ﷺ that they don't name their children "Muḥammad," as they believe that name is exclusive for Prophet ﷺ; instead they use the name, "Mehmet" because "Muḥammad" is reserved for only one. You can go through all of Turkey, from the Ottoman time until today, and you cannot find anyone with the name "Muḥammad," only "Mehmet." Out of respect they use that name exclusively for Prophet ﷺ.

So he entered that reality, the understanding and knowledge of *māʿrifatullāh*. *Lā ilāha illa-Llāh* takes you from *awḥāl ad-dunyā*, from the mud and dirt of this world, all the way from the *ḥarām*, forbidden, to the *ḥalāl*, Masjid al-Aqsā, where no sin can exist, as it is immediately burned. And that is why Hajj al-Bayt is important, because as soon as you go there you are cleaned. And it not only cleans you of past sins, but Allāh ﷻ, in His mercy, will clean your future sins also.

That is why He ordered one Hajj, as that *tajallī* with which He dresses you will not disappear; it is there and it takes you forward through all your life. That *Kalīmat at-Tawḥīd*, *lā ilāha illa-Llāh*, will take you, as Mawlana said, "All students who are making *dhikr* with *lā ilāha illa-Llāh* from one-hundred to a thousand times daily, even if they are not, will be dressed with that *tajallī* from the beginning of Ramadan, to be ready when Mahdī ؏ comes." So *lā ilāha illa-Llāh* takes us from the dirtiness of *dunyā* to begin our ascension into Heavens!

And when Prophet ﷺ went into Miʿrāj, where was his *ummah*? Did he leave it behind or they were with him? That is why in every level of Paradise he was asked, "Is he invited?" Of course when Paradise has been decorated, Allāh is inviting a guest! When they invite a president they fill the place with flags, ceremonies, and decorations. So when Allāh decorated Paradise, it means He invited a guest. Then why did the angels ask, "Has he been invited?" Because they saw the tail behind him! He brought behind him the *ummah*, those whom Allāh knows are of what kind; we are what we are!

Like children pleading with their father, "Don't leave us behind!" Prophet ﷺ brought the *ummah* behind him. Are they accepted? Yes, as whatever Prophet brings is accepted. In the first row are 124,000 *awlīyāullāh*, all of them with their sulṭān, may Allāh give him long life, and behind every *walī* are his *murīds*. So if you are president and take your son with you to meetings, can anyone say "no"? Today one Arab president brought his son with him to peace talks in Washington; can anyone say to him, "Don't bring your son!"

What about the Seal of Messengers ﷺ? Is he bringing one, or all of them? In *dunyā,* in his passing, and in his holy grave, he ﷺ said, "My *ummah,* my *ummah*!" On the Day of Judgment, he will say, "My *ummah,* my *ummah*!" And so Allāh is saying to him, "Don't go without taking them."

Everything in Dunya Is under Kalimat at-Tawhid

So *Kalīmat at-Tawḥīd* is an appearance of the Name that contains all possible existence. He didn't say what exists, but anything that you can imagine in your mind to exist in *dunyā,* all of it is under that Name. So when you say, *lā ilāha,* you are denying *dunyā,* to get away from it. Essentially, you are saying, "*Yā Rabbī*! We are not interested in these appearances of *dunyā,* as we used to run to it, and are wiping off the dust of human existence, *al-wujūd al-imkāni,* "the possible existence," as it is covering the Uniqueness of His Beautiful Name, "Allāh."

So *lā ilāha* denies everything of this dirty life and its dust, and affirms the existence of Allāh. So that is why it is two parts: "*lā ilāha*" and "*illa-Llāh.*" So *awlīyā* like us to enter the reality of that Name and reveal the lights Allāh is revealing to the heart of the believer. The "House of Allāh" is the heart of the believer. "Heaven and Earth cannot contain Me, but the heart of the believer can contain Me." So if we clean the walls of the heart, take away the dust of *dunyā* by saying, *lā ilāha,* and confirm Allāh's Manifestation by saying, *illa-Llāh,* that is what *awlīyāullāh* are trying to achieve. Mawlana Shaykh says, "That achievement has already been accepted by *awlīyā,* and they trust us with *lā ilāha illa-Llāh.*"

Sayyīdinā ʿAbd al-Qādir al-Jilānī ق, the *ghawth* of his time, said, "My feet are on the neck of every *walī.*" It has a meaning that we will not go into now. And we have to be careful, as Prophet ﷺ said, "Shayṭān never comes in my image." We have to believe fully what Prophet said, "Shayṭān can never cheat my servant by (disguising himself) using my image." Prophet is the only one who defeated his *shayṭān*, as he said in that *ḥadīth, ghalabtu shayṭānī,* when Jibrīl ﷺ opened his heart and took out the small black flesh that is the house of Shayṭān in everyone's heart. If you slaughter a cow, sheep or goat and look in the heart, you will see a small black clot; that is the entrance and home for Shayṭān in the heart. So the only one who defeated his *shayṭān* is

Prophet ﷺ, who said, "Whoever saw me in a dream is going to see me in reality."

And ʿAbd al-Qādir al-Jilānī ق said, "O *qawm*! Exhaust your *shayṭān* by *'ikhlāṣ*, sincerity, and by reading Sūrat al-'Ikhlāṣ." Say, *lā ilāha illa-Llāh*, and also recite:

Qul Hūwa Allāhu Āḥad Allāhu 'ṣ-Ṣamad lam yalid wa lam yūlad wa lam yakun lāhu kufūwan Āḥad.
Say, "He is Allāh, the Unique One! The Self-Sufficient Master, Whom all creatures need. He neither eats nor drinks. He begets not, nor was He begotten, and there is no one comparable or equal to Him!

(Sūrat al-'Ikhlāṣ 112: 1-4)

Sayyīdinā ʿAbd al-Qādir al-Jilānī ق said, *Lā ilāha illa-Llāh lā bi mujarrad al-lafdh bal maʿna al-haqiqi,* "It is not only by saying, *lā ilāha illa-Llāh* on the tongue, but by the reality in the heart. That is why we have to recite one-hundred to a thousand times, and that will burn Shayṭān from among the *jinn* and *ins* who are doing everything without limits. *annahu nāran,* it is fire to *shayāṭīn* and a light for believers."

Fire can burn fire; a huge fire takes over the smaller fire, which will disappear. So *lā ilāha illa-Llāh* is a big fire that takes Shayṭān's fire away and also your sins, and it is a light for *muwāhidūn*. The Sun is an example of that; the fire on the Sun gives us life. *Nār* becomes *diyā*, shining light, and it is fire but it gives you life. Without the Sun you cannot live. So that *lā ilāha illa-Llāh* will burn Shayṭān and become a light for believers.

Sayyīdinā ʿAbd al-Qādir al-Jilānī ق continues, "O my *ghulām*, my child! How dare you say, *lā ilāha illa-Llāh,* and in your heart there are too many *ilah* (gods)!" How do you say, "There is no god except Allāh," when your heart is full of gods and goddesses, and every sin is a god? Recite *lā ilāha illa-Llāh,* as that cleans the heart so well that you don't need any other cleaner. Anything that you depend on and trust other than Allāh is *sanamak,* your idol. Run away from the idols, and run to Allāh!"

Wa min Allāhi 't-tawfiq, bi ḥurmati 'l-ḥabīb, bi ḥurmati 'l-Fātiḥah.
And with Allāh is success. For the sake of the Beloved, for his sake we recite the opening chapter of Holy Qur'an.

The Reality of Tawhid, Allāh's Oneness

A'ūdhu billāhi min ash-Shayṭān ir-rajīm. Bismillāhi' r-Raḥmāni 'r-Raḥīm. Nawaytu 'l-arbā'īn, nawaytu 'l-'itikāf, nawaytu'l-khalwah, nawaytu 'l-'uzlah, nawaytu 'r-riyāḍa, nawaytu 's-sulūk, lillāhi Ta'alā fī hādhā 'l-masjid. Ati' ūllāh wa ati'ū 'r-Rasūl wa ūli 'l-amri minkum. (4:59)

Allāhummā sallī 'alā Sayyīdinā Muḥammad ḥattā yarda, Sayyīdinā Muḥammad. Allāhummā sallī 'alā Sayyīdinā Muḥammad. Lā ilāha illa-Llāh Muḥammadan Rasūlullāh. Qul "Allāh"! Awlīyā have many means to make their followers move like a rocket on the right path. Their track is always straight and the engine is always on the track. It is the main engine of the train, the locomotive, and it is very powerful, so anyone who jumps on it will arrive fast. That is why they ordered that every time you are in a meeting, you should make the *niyyah,* intention, that this meeting is your last, as your soul might be taken before the next meeting, so you should be in that meeting like someone expecting death.

Be one whose deeds are completely disconnected from *dunyā* by saying, *a'ūdhu billāhi min ash-Shayṭān ir-rajīm. Bismillāhi' r-Raḥmāni 'r-Raḥīm. Nawaytu 'l-arba'īn, nawaytu 'l-'itikāf, nawaytu 'l-khalwah, nawaytu 'l-'uzlah, nawaytu 'r-riyādah, nawaytu 's-sulūk, and nawaytu as-siyām,* to keep our *jawarih,* outside and inside, disconnected from *dunyā;* then you will receive the benefit as if you did seclusion for forty days!

Every time you sit for prayer or sit to give guidance for people for *Ākhirah,* then you will be written in the book. There is a book that everyone invents all kinds of ways to be mentioned in, *The Guinness Book of World Records.* Someone who ate 200 kilos of meat would be written in that book. And *awlīyā* have their heavenly book and give us hints what to say, so it will be written in that as if you did that *'amal.* So in every association you should intend, "We are making seclusion, or making disassociation with the world, to make movement to Allāh, and we are separating ourselves from talk of *dunyā.*" This way you cut Shayṭān to pieces!

It is said, "If you know Allāh, you know everything." If you have *mā'rifat* about your Lord, then that leads you to have *mā'rifat* of everything Allāh ﷻ wants you to know. And who knows himself knows his Lord, and who knows his limits stands by the limit of what Allāh orders him to do. Allāh sent messengers to put us on the track, so that when we reach the destination, pulled by that big engine to reach the door of *mā'rifat,* when you come to the door and knock, they will open it for you, as we mentioned in a previous session.

Prophet said, "I was given knowledge of *awwalīn wa 'l-ākhirīn*, what was and what will be.

One *walī*, ash-Shiblī ق, said, "For me, the Knowledge of Before and After is the knowledge of *Tawḥīd*, 'Oneness', and the knowledge of *Āḥadīyyah*, 'Uniqueness'." It is the cream of what the Prophet ﷺ came with. Why? Because it is *Maqām al-Hudūr*, "the Station of Presence," and *Maqām ash-Shuhūd*, "the Station of Vision."

So that is why we say, *Ḥuḍūr Allāh, Ḥuḍūr al-Ḥabīb, fanā'un fi-Llāh, Fanāun fi'l-Ḥabīb al-Musṭafā.* That means when you are in the State of Presence and Vision, and you are reciting *lā ilāha illa-Llāh,* you are in *Maqām at-Tawḥīd*. In the level of Oneness, *Tawḥīd*, you see everything is One. When you enter the *Maqām* of Vision, you enter the reality of the Beautiful Names and Attributes describing the Essence through the *dhikr* that reminds us of Allāh, *lā ilāha illa-Llāh.* The One of Whom we see the signs in *dunyā* is the One Whose Greatness we have to know in *Ākhirah*, Allāh. This *maqām* is *al-ḥuḍūr wa ash-shuhūd fi istighrāq fi nūrun rabbī.* You will be dipped in the Light of the Lord!

> *Allāhu nūru as-samāwāti wa al-arḍi mathalu nūrihi ka-mishkātin fīhā miṣbāḥun al-miṣbāḥu fi zujājatin az-zujājatu ka-'annahā kawkabun durrīyun yūqadu min shajaratin mubārakatin zaytūnatin lā sharqīyatin wa lā gharbīyatin yakādu zaytuhā yuḍī'u wa law lam tamsashu nār. Nūrun 'alā nūrin yahdīllāhu linūrihi man yashā'u wa yaḍribullāhu 'l-'amthāla li 'n-nāsi w 'Allāhu bi kulli shay'in 'Alīm.*
> *Allāh is the Light of the Heavens and the Earth. The parable of His Light is as a niche and within it a lamp, the lamp is in glass, the glass as it were a brilliant star, lit from a blessed tree, an olive, neither of the east nor of the west, whose oil would almost glow forth (of itself) although no fire touched it. Light upon Light! Allāh guides to His Light whom He wills. And Allāh sets forth parables for Mankind, and Allāh is Knower of all Things!*
>
> (Sūrat an-Nūr, 24:35)

Allāh is the Light of the Heavens and Earth: that level is *al-hidāya al-'uẓmā,* "the greatest guidance," *wal-maqām al-asna,* "and the highest level," *wal-hāl al-ḥusnā,* "and the most excellent of states," and *sa'adāt al-kubrā,* "the greatest happiness." So to be on that level is very simple; don't make it complicated. So many *awlīyā* have written about these stations, but if we say, *lā ilāha illa-Llāh,* we will reach the high levels that *awlīyā* reached! Some people are saying they cannot understand anything the *awlīyā* say, but we are speaking something to allow people to realize that Greatness, to give them a taste. It is *al-maqsad al-aqsa,* "the highest attainment," or "the highest state of excellence." It takes you to *qāba qawsayni aw adna,* "two bows' length or nearer," to be with Prophet ﷺ as a member of his *ummah,* from which he will not leave anyone behind.

Description of Haqiqat at-Tawhid

So what is *Ḥaqīqat at-Tawḥīd,* "the Reality of Tawḥīd"? For example, this element is one; it has no resemblance to anything else. That is unique in itself and in everything. No one resembles that: it is "one." That is why for Allāh to show you His Greatness and your uniqueness, He gave you a unique thumbprint that doesn't resemble anyone else's, to show that you don't resemble anyone. No one's heart resembles anyone else's, no kidney resembles another. Okay, there is some resemblance in organs; for example: when a doctor does a transplant, he has to make sure you have the right tissue type or the organ will be rejected.

So there are groupings of people, and they are not the same. He also makes groups to follow their own shaykh, not everyone follows one shaykh. Take *ḥikmah* from that, don't say, "My shaykh is higher than yours, my shaykh is the best." That is no *adab.* You have the same group, to be together, you have the same tissue type, but still that thumb doesn't resemble any other, not even if you are of the same tissue type. Also, Allāh created every leaf on a tree to not resemble any other leaf in size or composition or tissue type. Ask a scientist to do tests for you to prove this!

The word *"tawḥīd"* means that element has no resemblance. So when we understand that there is no resemblance and Who it is that has no resemblance: *qul Hūwa Allāhu Āḥad, Allāhu 'ṣ-Ṣamad.* Allāh is independent, and all Creation is dependent. Who is holding the universe together? If Allāh let it loose it will collapse, *bi ghayri 'amadin tarawnahā,* "with no pillars holding everything in space." Who can do that? Only Allāh! Compared to heavenly power and Allāh's Greatness, all their weapons are like toys. Allāh ﷻ is saying, "Everything that human beings have, We control!" Smart bombs and aircraft are like children's toys; if Allāh wills, in one second they disappear. If He says to the ocean to swallow all submarines and all vessels, what happens? They can disappear in one moment! May Allāh ﷻ protect us.

Look what happened (with the massive floods) in Pakistan, Allāh ﷻ punished everyone, and not all Pakistanis deserve that punishment. Like Sayyīdinā Mūsā, when he said, "*Yā Rabbī*! When You are angry with someone, why do You destroy the whole city. Why not just that one?" He spoke like that because He had familiarity with Allāh ﷻ. So Allāh said to him, "O Mūsā! Let me show you My Judgment. Go to that jungle and sit for a while." So he went there, waiting to see Allāh's Judgment. And he doesn't have patience, he is "*Kalīmullāh*," so among the *anbīyā* he feels some preference and higher distinction. So if he likes, like a child speaking to his father can say anything, it is accepted.

So Sayyīdinā Mūsā thinks he is better than anyone else, so he says as he likes, and he said, "How do you punish everyone who is innocent due to the acts of one person?" Allāh ﷻ left him waiting for three hours. He became impatient and said, "*Yā Rabbī*! What is this?" And as soon as he said that, many small ants crawled up his legs. Then Allāh ordered one ant to bite him and that ant was happy, as Allāh had ordered an ant to bite a prophet! That is love to Allāh and love to Sayyīdinā Mūsā.

Allāh commanded the ant, "Bite him very strongly!" As soon as he bit him, Sayyīdinā Mūsā pressed his leg and killed all the ants except a few. Then he heard a voice, "O Mūsā! What have you done?"

He said, "An ant bit me!"

"But you crushed all of them! That is My wisdom, one bad person among them causes all of them to be punished."

Those (flood victims in in Pakistan) who were innocent were given Paradise, and those who did wrong, the Hellfire is ready for them, but since they were punished they are sent to Paradise. Here is one message to Pakistanis from one of His *awlīyā*: "If you keep doing that, Allāh will continue to send like that." They blew up the *maqām* of one great *walī*, Sayyid ʿAlī Hujwiri ق! It is as Allāh said in *Ḥadīth Qudsī*:

Man ādha lī walīyyan ādhantahu bil-harb.

Who declares war on a Friend of Mine, I declare war on him.

Alā inna awlīyāullāh lā khawfan ʿalayhim wa lā hum yahzanūn.
Verily, on the Friends of Allāh there is no fear, nor shall they grieve.

(Sūrat Yūnus, 10:62)

So when they blew up that *maqām*, Allāh defended him. Sayyid 'Alī Hujwirī didn't want to defend himself, so Allāh defended him: He brought that huge flood. Twenty-five million for one. When they came to Sayyīdinā Lūt, the angels said, "We are coming by Allāh's order to destroy your people!" His people were gay. Anyone who protects gay people is going to get that punishment. We don't care about "freedom" or not, gay or not.

Allāh said to Sayyīdinā Lūt ☙, "Don't look behind you as you leave!" And in one strike He finished them, in one tornado or one hurricane; their homes were destroyed completely in one strike. So Allāh showed Sayyīdinā Mūsā, "For one, I take all!"

And that is Allāh's Uniqueness; no one can be like that. And how to save ourselves? By *Kalīmat at-Tawḥīd, lā ilāha illa-Llāh*. When we recite that we are saying, "There is no one to resemble You, *yā Rabbī*!" And that is *Maqām al-Huḍūr* and *Maqām ash-Shuhūd*, the Station of Presence and the Station of Seeing. To those doing their *dhikr,* Allāh will open these veils, slowly, slowly, for them to see this beauty.

So the *Maqām at-Tawḥīd* is a level of beauty. Every year they have a beauty contest broadcast on different TV stations. One is chosen as the most beautiful and is crowned, and I don't know what else she gets of jewelry, watches, and that person becomes so highly respected, for nothing! What do you think about the One Who created beauty? When you enter yourself by saying, *lā ilāha illa-Llāh,* He will dress you with heavenly beauty. He will be happy to bring you to His Heavenly Creation and say to them, "Look! These are my beautiful ones that have separated themselves from Shayṭān!" even if you only say it once a day, or even once in your life. So one recitation of *lā ilāha illa-Llāh* is enough for one day, and for one moment. Say, "*lā ilāha illa-Llāh*"; it is describing The One Who has no resemblance!

> *Qul Hū Allāhu Āḥad,* "Say (O Muḥammad), 'He is Allāh, (the) One!'" *Allāhu 'ṣ-Ṣamad,* "The Self-Sufficient Master, Whom all creatures need; He neither eats nor drinks." *Lam yalid wa lam yūlad,* "He begets not, nor was He begotten," *walam yakun lāhu kufūwan Āḥad,* "And there is none equal or comparable to Him."   (Sūrat al-'Ikhlāṣ, 112: 1-4)

And the meaning of "Allāh ☙ is One" is, He is denying the division of His Essence. *Nafiy al-inqisam fī dhātihi,* "There is no partner with Me and no division in Me." That One has no partner other than Him, and He is the One that looks like no one. He is Creator, and we are His servants and His Creation.

Who Has the Highest Intelligence?

Sayyīdinā Junayd al-Baghdādī ق said, *Idhā tanā 'uqūl al-'uqalā ila 't-tawḥīd intihā il al-ḥīrā.* "The brains of the most intelligent men who have brains..." as not everyone has brains, those who have '*dunyā* brains' are considered to have no brain, as to Allāh said *dunyā* is not valued the weight of a mosquito's wing. So why have a brain for it? That means when you add all such brains together they don't weigh the wing of a mosquito, if you still say, "I am here."

Sayyīdinā Junayd ق said, "The highest of brains that understand are the *awlīyā*'s; whatever heights *awlīyā* can reach, they have the greatest intelligence as they have left *dunyā*. If we add all the intelligence of *awlīyā* with all their heavenly knowledge, and we add together their farthest possible goal in understanding Divine Oneness, they will be stunned and in bewilderment. *Ḥīra* means "they are bewildered". They reached that level of astonishment where they cannot comprehend. With all the *tawḥīd* they have made, they reached the Ocean of Bewilderment and they cannot swim in it. They must reach their limits!" That means that anyone who says, *lā ilāha illa-Llāh* one day reaches the Level of Bewilderment, in which there is no way to understand anything except traces of that Reality.

Sayyīdinā Junayd also said, *Tandarisu fīhi al-'ulūm wa yabqā 'Llāh ka lam yazal,* "*Tawḥīd* means in it are all the images of Creation, and in it all the images of Creation disappear! Say, *lā ilāha illa-Llāh,* and everything disappears, and you get the reward of that, as all of Creation recites *lā ilāha illa-Llāh,* and all of that is written for you! The recitation of all creatures, deserts, sands, and particles, saying *lā ilāha illa-Llāh,* is written for you! All Creation is disappearing in that ocean and all knowledge stops and we cannot understand anymore."

That is why you say, 'I am standing, *yā Rabb,* at my limits.' And that is why you know you can go no further. And Allāh's Essence stays as it is, unchanged. We cannot say anything about 'it'. We don't know what to say, in Arabic there is no word to express 'it.'

And they said that the best of what has been said about *tawḥīd* is what Abū Bakr aṣ-Ṣiddīq ق said, "*SubhānAllāh,* Praise be to Allāh that He did not create a way for His Creation to know Him."

You cannot stand beside the Divine Presence, and that is your limit of knowledge; you cannot go in. That is the limit of knowledge. You are a particle in an ocean, so what do you know about *tawḥīd*? "Praise be to the One who didn't provide a means for Creation to know Him!" How do you know Him? By realizing your *inability* to know Him! "I am coming with complete *ajaz,* inability. With that inability, I know my inability to know You." You have to declare that you cannot know or understand the level of *tawḥīd.* If you cannot understand *tawḥīd,* how can you understand Maqām adh-Dhāt, the "Station of the Name 'Allāh'"? If you cannot understand *lā ilāha illa-Llāh,* which is *Maqām at-Tawḥīd,* how you can understand "Allāh"? So we can only follow the way of Prophet ﷺ, then you will be there:

> *Qul in kuntum tuḥibbūn-Allāha fattabiʿūnī yuḥbibkumu Allāhu wa yaghfir lakum dhunūbakum w'Allāhu Ghafūru 'r-Raḥīm.*
> *Say, "If you love Allāh, follow me (Muḥammad). Allāh will love you and forgive you your sins, for Allāh is Oft-Forgiving, Most Merciful."*
> (Sūrat 'Āli ʿImrān, 3:31)

So our duty is to follow, and to know our limits and not to trespass them. Today they come to you with all kinds of ways of expressing themselves and say, "We are one, we are united." United with whom? With Shayṭān. How can you declare you are united with Allāh; that is *kufr*! You cannot even understand *tawḥīd.* Sayyīdinā Abū Bakr aṣ-Ṣiddīq ق said you cannot, or you will completely disappear. "Glory to the One who did not give a way to know about Him, except by our complete inability to know Him!" Declare that! Don't say "I"!

Wa qīla fit-tawḥīd, and it is said that *tawḥīd* means to deny three words ending with *"yā,"* the last letter of the Arabic alphabet. There are all kinds of knowledge between *"alif,"* the first letter of the Arabic alphabet, which declares Allāh's Oneness in its standing up, and *"yā"*. So that means all knowledge is between *"alif"* and *"yā."*

So if you want to understand Oneness, drop the *yā;* this leaves *alif,* and that is in three words. First is *"lī" (lam yā),* which in Arabic means, "belonging to Me," and yet, you don't own anything. You go to the grave and if you have a ring they take it, and they take everything from you, and wrap you in the shroud and throw you in, then the one who digs the grave comes and if you have any gold teeth, he steals them also, and they take your organs and sell them. You are gone and no one cares how you are cut into pieces.

First is, *lā taqul lī,* "Don't say, 'it belongs to me'." And second, don't say, *bī,* "through me". "You are something because of me!" Or don't say, "I am existing, I am president," "I am king!" What for? Kings don't die? Then what do you think you are? Nothing. Third, don't say, *minnī,* "from me". So *lī, bī* and *minnī,* don't say them. (Note: These three Arabic words all end in the suffix *yā,* in these cases pronounced '*ī*'.) Say, "It is from Him to Him," or, *minka wa ilayk,* "from You to You (Allāh); there is nothing in our hands!" Then you will be saved.

May Allāh ﷻ forgive us and may Allāh ﷻ bless us.

Wa min Allāhi 't-tawfiq, bi ḥurmati 'l-ḥabīb, bi ḥurmati 'l-Fātiḥah.
And with Allāh is success. For the sake of the Beloved, for his sake we recite the opening chapter of Holy Qur'an.

Five Principles of Maqam at-Tawhid

A'ūdhu billāhi min ash-Shayṭān ir-rajīm. Bismillāhi' r-Raḥmāni 'r-Raḥīm.
Nawaytu 'l-arbā'īn, nawaytu 'l-'itikāf, nawaytu'l-khalwah, nawaytu 'l-'uzlah,
nawaytu 'r-riyāḍa, nawaytu 's-sulūk, lillāhi Ta'alā fī hādhā 'l-masjid.
Ati' ūllāh wa ati'ū 'r-Rasūl wa ūli 'l-amri minkum. (4:59)

When one says, *lā ilāha illa-Llāh,* he is denying everything in this *dunyā* and confirming *illa-Llāh,* the Greatness of the Creator. *Awlīyāullāh* say not only are they denying what is in *dunyā,* but also they are not even looking at what is in *Ākhirah,* as what they like is only to be in the Divine Presence. To them there is nothing except Allāh's existence and nothing else for them exists, as Rābi'ah al-'Adawiyyah said, "O Allāh! I am not worshipping You for Paradise and not from fear of Hellfire, but I am worshipping You for You Only!"

Today they have taught them, not tasty Sufi speech on their tongues, but to say always "I," or "my students," "my this and that". It is better to say "our". People might say, "Why use plural?" That is because it avoids selfishness and egoism. When you say "we" it is many people, but "I" is one person. Today they put this in their heads with technology. Today there is the iPhone (ego phone) and the iPad. Why didn't they write "eyePhone"? That is Shayṭān always making us say, "I". As we said before, in *Maqāmāt at-Tawḥīd,* you have to drop the three *ya's*: *"lī, wa bī, wa minnī". Lī* means, "for me," *bī* means, "by me" or "through me," and *minnī* means, "from me." That means everything, "from me" and "to me". No, it is "from You to You, *yā Rabbī*! My appearance in this *dunyā* is from You, and my bad *'amal* is from me, and my good *'amal* is from You!"

Don't say everything is "from me." Allāh ﷻ said in Holy Qur'an, 'Who cares for my wife and my children? Only myself.' Those are the traces that go with you all the way to Day of Judgment. Prophet ﷺ doesn't say "myself," but he says, "*ummati,* my nation," and *awlīyā* say "my students" to take to the presence of Prophet ﷺ.

Yawm yafirru 'l-marru min akhīhi wa ummihi wa abīhi wa ṣāḥibatihi wa banīh. likull imrin yawmaydhin shānun yughnīh.

On the Day when a man flees from his brother, and his mother, and his father, and his wife, and his children! Every man that Day will have concern enough to make him heedless (of others). (Sūrat ʿAbasa, 80:34-37)

Likull imrin yawmaydhin shānun yughnīh. Everyone is fearful for himself, if he is going to be punished or not, and it is a fearful day! "On that Day everyone must follow My Prophet. Follow the Way I showed through My messengers." *Wa yawma yufirru min akhīhi wa ummihi wa abīhi wa ṣāḥibatihi, wa banīh.* "When you run away from your brother and father and mother and your wife and your children, also you run away from them in *dunyā* when you are busy with Your Lord!" You want to be cleaned in *dunyā* of everything but attachment to Allāh.

That is why they went to Rābiʿah al-ʿAdawiyyah ﷺ and said, "Why don't you marry?" she said, "I don't have time." She ran away. Even though it is an Islamic obligation, after her husband died she ran from her family, saying, "I am busy repenting to my Lord. My *istighfār* needs another *istighfār* to be accepted." As she did 100 *istighfār*, it came to her heart that they were not accepted and she did another 100 *istighfār* to make the previous *istighfār* accepted.

So never say *lī*, "to me," and never say *bī*, "by me" and never say *minnī*, "from me." It is more respectful to speak in the third person; it is higher *adab. Man waqaʿ bi bihār at-tawḥīd ma yazdad fi ayāmin illa murūr ʿatasha,* "Who falls or leaves everything and left the love of *dunyā* behind his back." These are *awlīyāullāh*; they jump into the sweet oceans of *tawḥīd*, unity, where you will never quench your thirst; you will always be thirsty, like someone who is taking salt and is always thirsty.

That is why of the five pillars of Islam—*Shahādah, Ṣalāt, Zakāt, Hajj* and fasting in Ramadan—in the last you get thirsty. Allāh ﷻ said, *ramadun lī wa 'anā ajzī bih,* "Ramadan is for Me; you are fasting for Me and getting thirsty for Me in Oneness Oceans. I will dip you in and dress you in oceans of *tawḥīd*." Allāh ﷻ, in His wisdom, made us feel that thirst in our day in order to be *sabab.* This causes anyone fasting Ramadan to be dipped in the Ocean of Oneness without feeling anything.

On the Day of Judgment, he will come out dressed in that dress of a real *muwwāḥid*, not a fake *muwwāḥid* who professes by tongue only. You are a real one, as you were dipped in the Ocean of Oneness. That is big and not small; that is something you cannot understand. You are going to be dressed by Allāh ﷻ in the dress of *tawḥīd. Aynas-sāimūn,* "They will be called, 'Where are those who are fasting?' and they will enter a door to Paradise called *'ar-Rayyān,'* which means, 'quenched thirst.'" *Awlīyā* like to quench their thirst in the oceans of *tawḥīd,* to appear as a *walī* on the Day of Judgment. And you don't know you are a *walī.*

Shaykh al-Husayri ﷺ said there are five principles in *tawḥīd*: *Raf' al-ḥadath,* the same word used for the shower you take after you experience carnal desires, but it has a different meaning. It means that Allāh ﷻ does not increase or decrease. *Ḥadath* is something that happens daily. For example, you go to work, you meet a person, or you're given a higher rank. Your life is changing, you are becoming older day after day. *Raf' al-ḥadath* means "to keep in mind that Allāh ﷻ never changes." He is Allāh, not more and not less. The second principle is, *wa ifrād ul-qidam,* meaning, "There is only One that is post-Eternal, ancient, the only One that is today as He will be tomorrow, only One that never changes, without beginning or end." These two are very important: there are no changes for Allāh ﷻ, He is as He was before, now and forever; and, He is the only One like that.

The third principle is *hajur al-ikhwān,* to be away from everyone else, "Leave the *ikhwān* and come to My Door. Don't look behind you." An example is, Sayyīdinā Bayāzīd al-Bistāmi ق was walking with his followers when he saw a lady coming from the other side, and as soon as they approached he hugged her. They were near a house and he entered the house with the lady and closed the door. His followers fell into speculation, saying, "What happened? Is this the conduct of a *walī*? This is not a *walī,* he did something wrong." Except there was one person, who stood at the door waiting for his shaykh to come out.

Sayyīdinā Bayāzīd said, "What are you doing, my son?"

He said, "I am waiting to do *khidmah.*"

"Where are your brothers?"

He said, "My job is only to be waiting, ready to serve you, and it is not my job to know what my brothers are doing. My entire focus is on you, exclusively!"

Sayyīdinā Bayāzīd ق said, "Come inside, my son. The others had bad thoughts, but this is my sister. You are the only one that understood and you didn't mind whether this was my sister or not. You were only concerned about when I would open the door and when you could do *khidmah*. Bring two witnesses and marry my sister."

So that *murīd* became his *khalīfah*. This is a very important lesson: don't play with *awlīyā*! If that happened to us, we would only look backward (to find dirt), to backbite as much as we could. *Hajur al-ikhwān* is to be concerned with only yourself, not with others.

The fourth principle is *mufāraqat al-awṭān*, "to leave your birth country or what you inhabit"; leave your "inn," and to go to *Maqām at-Tawḥīd*, which is *lā ilāha illa-Llāh*. The Prophet ﷺ said, *ḥubb al-awṭān min al-īmān*. "Love of country is from faith," but you try to leave even that. You want no connection to the country to which you are going, so most of your connections are to the country from where you came. They ask, "What is your *waṭan* (nation)?" *Waṭṭin qahrabā al-manzil*, "Find a house to put your electricity or telephone bill." *Waṭṭin* means "find a bank" to pay your bills today. You don't have to go every month to pay, but you find a house to take that responsibility. Separate with all these connections to the *waṭan* you inhabit.

Also, your soul inhabits your body, so it means, "Leave your ego and free your soul from your connection to the desires of the body." Today people are so connected to their bodies and how beautiful they look, jogging, going to the gym, where there are too many *shayṭāns*! Why do they want to become healthy?

La yastākhirūna sa'atan wa lā yastaqdimūn, "For every nation there is a time to go," and every person is a *waṭan*, nation. Each cell in the body is like a huge factory, with its own defenses and production. Allāh ﷻ counted them and knows everything about every cell, and they are all coming to His Presence on the Day of Judgment. Don't jog and go to hell's gyms. As it says in the first verse we read, you are not going to be delayed one hour or moved forward one hour. If you run from here to Antarctica, you are not decreasing or increasing your life. Don't bother to run, but also don't judge those who are running because Allāh ﷻ made them run, to make them healthy. And if you don't run, then Allāh ﷻ made you like that, to be healthy in that way.

People are judging each other, and they are coming to me and complaining. Why? Allāh knows what is with you and what is not with you!

The fifth and last principle is, *wa nusyan mā 'ulim*, "to forget what is known". Whatever you have achieved in your *dunyā*, forget about it as it will not benefit you. That is why *awlīyā* forget about *dunyā*. They live in the moment and they don't mention what was before, like someone who lost their memory; *awlīyā* have heavenly Alzheimer's Syndrome! Don't bother with it, but bother yourself to say, *Lā ilāha illa-Llāh. Dunyā* keeps you from seeing *shawāriq al-anwār*, the sunrise of heavenly lights.

Sayyīdinā Abdul Qadir al-Jilani, the *ghawth* of his time, may Allāh sanctify his soul, said, "How dare you say, *lā ilāha illa-Llāh,* when your heart is full with many *'ilāhs,'* gods!"

For a *walī* to say that is big. *Kayfa taqūlulā ilāha illa-Llāh wa qalba mamlu' bil aliha,* "How are you sanctifying and praising; how are you worshipping?" Because you are not saying, *lā ilāha illa-Llāh* in a real sense; it is blended with the idols within you! It is like you are really saying, "there is no *ilah*" except you, like the Quraysh before Islam worshipped their idols. Don't say to your idols, "There is no god except you, my idols!"

Sayyīdinā Abdul Qadir was saying, "Don't put any statues in your heart." Love of money and love of self are statues that block the real *tawḥīd. Lā yanfa'uk tawḥīd al-lisān wa anta 'ala shirk,* "It is not only speaking of papers, but when *awlīyā* speak, they dress us with whatever they are speaking." Sayyīdinā Abdul Qadir al-Jilani ق said that, to dress anyone who reads that and to take out the statues of the heart and replace them with the real meaning of *lā ilāha illa-Llāh.*

Awlīyā are not playing! They remind you about your mistakes, but they also take away the wrong you are doing. The normal scholar will remind you, but will not take away that mistake of having idols in your heart. That will not give you benefit, but it is like making prayer on a dirty carpet; you must first clean it. So it will not benefit you to have a correct word with a dirty heart. For *awlīyā*, dirtiness is not love of *dunyā;* they already left that. For them, dirtiness is love of *Ākhirah,* as Rābi'ah al- 'Adawiyyah ﵂ said, "O Allāh! I am not worshipping You for love of Paradise nor from fear of Hell, but for love of You!"

That is the reality of love, not like the standard cliché, "Islam is peace and love." The reality of love is to go through the path to *mā'rifatullāh,* and then you see what people cannot see and hear what people cannot hear.

An example is, even if you bring all the best singers and musicians in this world, they cannot be compared with the singing of one angel. When you begin to say truly, *lā ilāha illa-Llāh,* the *taṣbīḥ* of angels comes to your ears and you become drunk from it! It is said that if one *ḥūrī* of Paradise would show her finger, from the beauty of her finger and its beautiful perfume, all in *dunyā* would faint! What is perfume? Today they sell you tons of perfumes, but *awlīyā* give you real perfume: to say, *lā ilāha illa-Llāh*

Muḥammadun Rasūlullāh. You cannot say *lā ilāha illa-Llāh* without saying *Muḥammadun Rasūlullāh*. That is our safety. Whoever wants to get upset about this, let them do so!

Sayyīdinā Abdul Qadir al-Jilani ق said, *Al-qalb al-muwwāḥid yudnī shayṭān*, "The heart that is always mentioning the Oneness of Allāh will exhaust his *shayṭān*." The one whose heart is always in *tawḥīd*, always saying, *"lā ilāha illa-Llāh"*, that one's *shayṭān* will become exhausted. That is killing him and it is a sword against him. The *mushrik yudnihi shayṭān*, the one who associates partners with Allāh ﷻ, that *shirk* will make his *shayṭān* exhausted. Don't say, "I am not *mushrik*." Yes, we are. "Of course we are not *mushrik*! We are Muslims!"

But that is not what Sayyīdinā Abdul Qadir ق is saying. He is saying that the heart that has no one other than Allāh ﷻ will harm his *shayṭān*. The heart that doesn't mention any except Allāh, and the full heart that is in that *tawḥīd* makes his *shayṭān* exhausted. But the one who makes his heart open for all kinds of worldly desires, and also heavenly desires, that heart is making partnership with Allāh ﷻ so his Shayṭān will exhaust him.

That is why Muslims are exhausted today: we are molding clay, which is *dunyā*, with pure heavenly Paradise elements, trying to mold a statue. That is why our prayers have to be only for Allāh ﷻ.

> *Qul innamā anā basharun mithlukum yūhā ilayya annamā ilāhukum ilāhun wāhidun faman kāna yarjū liqā rabbihi falya'mal 'amalan sālihan wa lā yushrik bi-'ibādati rabbihi 'aḥada.*
> *Say (O Muḥammad), "I am only a man like you. It has been inspired to me that your God is One God (Allāh), so whoever hopes for the Meeting with his Lord, let him work righteousness and associate none as a partner in the worship of his Lord."* (Sūrat al-Kahf, 18:110)

Prophet ﷺ is so humble! With all that Allāh ﷻ gave him, he said only, "But I am different in that it is revealed to me." What is different? That means a huge difference, someone who can receive *wahī.*

Prophet ﷺ is telling us, "Don't worship nicely and then run to your work and not keep worship in your heart." Deal with *dunyā* matters, yes, but don't leave worship from your heart. The one who likes to meet with His Lord on the Day of Judgment, let him do a good *'amal.* What is that? To put no partner with His Lord. Don't put yourself with your Lord, saying, "I am an engineer, I am a doctor, I am a carpenter." Do you do that? Your honor is not with what you do, nor from any degree, but only Allāh's honor is what counts! Can you go to Allāh ﷻ on Judgment Day and when you are called, you say, "O, my Lord! Wait one second, I have a Master's degree!"

What does it say in Holy Qur'an about those who refute *'Ism adh-Dhāt*?

Qul Allāh thumma dharhum fi khawdihim yal'abūn.
Say, "Allāh," then leave them to play in their vain discussions.

(Sūrat al-'An'ām, 6:91)

"Say 'Allāh' and leave them in their playing." They say, "Don't say, 'Allāh,'" so then what else is there to say, "Shayṭān"? What should you say when you have a problem? Do you say, "O Hollywood!"

Wa mā Muḥammadun illa rasūl. qad khalat min qablihi 'r-rusūl. Afa in māta aw qutil anqalabtum 'alā ā'aqābikum wa man yanqalib 'alā 'aqibayhi falan yadurra allāha shayān wa sayajzī'Llāhu 'sh-shākirīn.
Muḥammad is no more than a messenger; many messengers passed away before him. If he died or were slain, will you then turn back on your heels (as disbelievers)? And he who turns back on his heels, not the least harm will he do to Allāh, and Allāh will reward to those who are grateful.

(Sūrat 'Āli 'Imrān, 3:144)

How to Know You Reached Maqam at-Tawhid

At the Station of *Qāba Qawsayn*, Prophet ﷺ saw Allāh ﷻ. "We have not yet reached *Maqām at-Tawḥīd*; the only one to reach it is the Prophet ﷺ." He is the only one to reach the Divine Presence, the reality of reaching *qāba qawsayni aw adna*! And the *mushrik*, who puts partnership of *dunyā* with *Ākhirah*, is not yet outside *awhāl ad-dunyā* and will be exhausted by Shayṭān. There is not one person outside that, even who has ten or one-hundred billion dollars, multiple luxury homes and cars. Everyone has a problem and no one can say, "I have no problem," because Allāh ﷻ is teaching you that when you have problems you should remember Him, but you don't.

When you have no problems, you reached *Maqām at-Tawḥīd*; like *awlīyāullāh* don't care about *dunyā*, who dies, dies. What is better, to be in *dunyā* or *Ākhirah*? So if someone comes to a *walī* and says, "I am sick, I am in a problem. Make *du'ā*." What *du'ā*? Go to *Ākhirah*, it is better. But with their mercy they make *du'ā*, and their *du'ā* is strong.

May Allāh ﷻ cure us and take away the *shirk* from our hearts! Say, *lā ilāha illa-Llāh*. Say, *Bismillāhi' r-Raḥmāni 'r-Raḥīm*. Say, *Qul Hū Allāhu 'Āḥad* (*Sūrat al-Ikhlāṣ*). If you recite these daily you will be saved, despite whatever comes from difficulties and miseries. The *awlīyā* dress you with the reality of *tawḥīd*. They are not like you. They don't speak to give you advice. Even if no one says, *"lā ilāha illa-Llāh"* and no one says *Sūrat al-Ikhlāṣ*, they dress you. They already have the dress and they dress you one by one. Whether you do this or not, they have to dress you because you took their hands in *baya'*, so they are under that responsibility. They have to dress you as they are responsible in presence of Prophet ﷺ.

Ghawth, Quṭb, *Nujabā*, *Nuqabā*, *Awtād*, and *Akhyār* are different types of *awlīyā* that support servants of an-Nabī. They cannot leave you without clothes. Can you walk naked in the street? Someone will come and dress you, since we are all naked in *dunya*, from making a partnership of *dunyā* and *Ākhirah*. They dress you in prepared dresses.

According to the *walī's* level you get a dress, and the higher level has a higher dress, *wa fawqa kulli dhi 'ilmin 'alīm*, "Above every knower is a (higher) knower," (Sūrah Yūsuf, 12:76) until you reach *Sulṭān al-Awlīyā*. When he dresses you, then Prophet ﷺ will dress you and that dress is far higher than what the Sultan dresses.

May Allāh ﷻ forgive us and bless us and we will continue at Fajr, *inshā'Allāh*. We remind everyone that we began that series to explain what we know in Islam. It is not, as they say, that there is no hierarchy. In fact there is a reality of a pyramid and a hierarchy and *awlīyāullāh* have different things they do and duties. As of today we have made 23 or 24 *suḥbahs*, all of them to describe what these *awlīyāullāh* do, to describe the *ghawth*, what he does and to describe these five groups of *awlīyāullāh*. And then we come to the senior Muslims in these communities, to shed a light on this knowledge that no one is touching today.

Today what are they discussing? Only politics, as if the only concern is *dunyā* and nothing else. Mosques are used to promote political agendas. You can rent a hall and speak about what you want, but speak about *Ākhirah* in the mosque, not politics or *dunyā* matters. Why do you bring such subjects to the podium of the mosque?

Al-masājidu lillāh.
The mosques are for Allāh. (Sūrat al-Jinn 72:18)

In the mosque, don't speak about what the president or the cabinet did, or about foreign policy, or what is or is not our right. The *masjid* is for worship! There you read Qur'an and *ḥadīth*, pray, and do *dhikr*. Don't make *halaqa* circles under false pretenses, to recruit people for evil, saying, "I like *jihad* and want to save the *ummah*." You are putting the *ummah* in difficulties and problems! Mosques are Allāh's Houses, so don't make partnership with Him by bringing something dirty there!

May Allāh ﷻ forgive us and may Allāh ﷻ bless us.

a min Allāhi 't-tawfīq, bi ḥurmati 'l-ḥabīb, bi ḥurmati 'l-Fātiḥah.
And with Allāh is success. For the sake of the Beloved, for his sake we recite the opening chapter of Holy Qur'an.

Maqam al-Ikhlas, the Level of Sincerity

A'ūdhu billāhi min ash-Shayṭān ir-rajīm. Bismillāhi' r-Raḥmāni 'r-Raḥīm. Nawaytu 'l-arbā'īn, nawaytu 'l-'itikāf, nawaytu'l-khalwah, nawaytu 'l-'uzlah, nawaytu 'r-riyāḍa, nawaytu 's-sulūk, lillāhi Ta'alā fī hādhā 'l-masjid. Ati' ūllāh wa ati'ū 'r-Rasūl wa ūli 'l-amri minkum. (4:59)

As we said before, the heart that keeps declaring and manifesting the Oneness of Allāh ﷻ, *Maqām at-Tawḥīd*, that person and that heart will make his Shayṭān exhausted. And the one who is always associating himself with Allāh ﷻ, who whatever he does of good he says, "I did that, I gave money, I gave a donation for Pakistan."

It is as if Pakistan became a commercial for everything, for violence, for disasters. I don't know what is happening in Pakistan. It might be there are too many *mushriks* there, too many people calling others to themselves. There is too much black magic there! I didn't see a Pakistani that didn't say, "I have black magic." It is rare to find someone who doesn't have black magic in Kenya, Ghana, Indonesia, etc., where there is so much black magic. May Allāh take away that black magic!

It is worthless when they use it on human beings. Black magic is really Shayṭān preventing you from declaring *tawḥīd*. So the one who is prevented from *tawḥīd* will be exhausted by Shayṭān. So what do you need? You need sincerity. When we have sincerity then we are going to throw out Shayṭān from our hearts. And how you can achieve sincerity?

> *Yā ayyuhal-ladhīna āmanū ittaqūllāh wa kūnū ma' aṣ-ṣādiqīn.*
> *O you who believe! Fear Allāh and be with those who are pious (in word and deed).* (Sūrat at-Tawbah, 9:119)

Those who have *taqwā*, piety, what is Allāh telling them? You must have *taqwā*, otherwise it is a waste of time. When you have *taqwā*, He allows you to be with trustworthy people to take you forward. So be with these trustworthy people, who kept their covenant with Allāh and never changed. *Taqwā* is to be steadfast, and we are struggling with that.

The Power of Ikhlas Sharifah

How do we achieve *ikhlāṣ*? In the Holy Qur'an there is a chapter, "*al-Ikhlāṣ*" that begins with, "*Qul Hūwa Allāhu 'Āḥad.*" If you want to achieve sincerity, read *Ikhlāṣ Sharīfah*. That is why *awlīyāullāh* order their followers to read *Sūrat al-Ikhlāṣ* 100 to 1,000 times daily. When someone has a problem and I say, "Read '*yā Fattah*' 100 times," they say, "daily?" What do you mean? Do you want it monthly or yearly? It is too much for them! We are busy. In what? Busy in business. So read *Sūrat al-Ikhlāṣ*; it will become manifest in you. When you are coming to Allāh reciting *Sūrat al-Ikhlāṣ*, do you think He will throw you out? If someone is knocking at your door and you say, "I am not answering," if that person is persistent, what will you do eventually? You open the door; either you shout at him or you welcome him. Allāh is not like us. His door is from east to west, and if you want to go out, there is no way. That 'exit' is like the eye of a needle! Then He will manifest on you the *barakah* of the holy chapter, *Sūrat al-Ikhlāṣ*.

But Shayṭān makes us unaware of *Sūrat al-Ikhlāṣ*. If you go to a rich man, or a president or king, they give you medallions, showing his generosity. You come a second time, he gives another medallion. You come a third time, he might not invite you again1 When you make *salām* to Prophet ﷺ, he will answer you with a better *salām*. Whoever makes one *ṣalawāt* on Prophet ﷺ, Allāh makes ten *ṣalawāt* on that person. Allāh's *ṣalawāt* on that person is far greater, even there is no description of it!

The *Ṣaḥābah* ؓ used to pass by Prophet ﷺ and say, "*As-salāmu 'alayk, yā Rasūlullāh,*" and he replied, "*Wa 'alaykum as-salām wa raḥmatullāh, yā 'abdAllāh!*" And then that *Ṣaḥābī* ؓ would pass another time and get another *salām* from Prophet ﷺ. *Ṣaḥābah* showed that sincerity by sending *salām* on Prophet ﷺ. And we are sending *salām* on Prophet ﷺ from here, *as-salātu was-salām 'alayk, yā Rasūlullāh* ﷺ! Do you think Prophet ﷺ is not answering? Of course he is! There are about 100 people here. So ten multiplied by 100 equals 1,000. Each one will get 1,000 *ḥasanāt*. And if there are 5,000 people you will get 50,000 *ḥasanāt*. If you want to get that benefit, go to Indonesia, where there are at least 5,000 to 10,000 attendees at every mosque!

So whoever comes with sincerity, with *Qul Hūwa Allāhu 'Āḥad*, the door is open. Sincerity is the pulp of all sayings and actions, *af'al*. That is the secret and the main seed of sincerity. It is the fruit that has the *qushr*, shell, of your sayings and your actions. The indication of sincerity is what appears or manifests through your sayings, what you speak and how you act. If you speak well and are respectful to everyone, that indicates sincerity. Sincerity is to be patient with the one you don't like, with whom you can never meet eye to eye, and that is very difficult. There it shows sincerity, as he is Allāh's servant also. Allāh sent him as a test for you to see how you are going to take it.

To save the fruit you need the shell, and to save your sincerity you need a shell, which is the actions and sayings. Whatever is inside manifests in the shell. If the fruit inside is rotten, then the shell is finished as well. So the shell must not be rotten, meaning, your actions and saying must be of a higher level. How do you speak to someone important? Very nicely, so that you can attract them towards you. How do you speak to Allāh and then to Prophet ﷺ? It is important to stand when Prophet ﷺ is being mentioned. Here we would be standing and sitting without end, but people are not accustomed to it. Therefore, stand in your heart. People ask me, "Is there a problem? Why are these people standing and sitting?" What should I say? So, be normal.

Sincerity is the fruit, and if there is no sincerity, then what do you have inside? What do you do with a dry shell? You don't throw it; it is something important. What you do with it? You burn it. Burn your bad actions and your bad sayings. Punishment is to clean and Hellfire is to burn bad actions and to keep the pulp clean. Try to throw away your bad actions and bad sayings from yourself.

Listen, O Believer! O *Muwwāḥid*! *Allāh* said in the Holy Qur'an:

Rabbu 'l-māshriqi wa 'l-māghrib fattakhidh-hu wakīla.
(He is) Lord of the East and the West. There is no god but He. Take Him therefore (as your) Disposer of Affairs. (Sūrat al-Muzzammil, 73:9)

Be careful, He is the Creator of East and West, but there is a meaning here. Yes, He is the Creator of the beginning of the sunrise, *shawāriq al-anwār*, the rising lights. He is the Creator of the rising lights and Creator of the setting lights. But it is immediately followed by *lā ilāha illa-Hūwa,* bringing your attention to what is much deeper. *Lā ilāha illa-Llāh* means, "There is no Creator except Allāh." *lā ilāha illā Hūwa* means, "There is no Creator except the Unknown Essence."

That is *'Ism adh-Dhāt,* which is *qul Hūwa,* before *"Allāh,"* meaning, "more Unknown." So if He is Lord of East and West, then He is the One that is Unknown. Even the light of east and west goes down, but His Essence is Unknown.

And then He said:

Rabbu 'l-mashriqayn wa rabbu 'l-maghribayni fa bi ayyi ālāi rabbikumā tukadhdhibān. (He is) Lord of the two Easts and Lord of the two Wests. Then which of the favors of your Lord will you deny? (Sūrat ar-Raḥmān, 55:17-18)

"He is the Lord of the two Easts and the two Wests." Why are you lying about Allāh ﷻ? Is there more than one east, one west, and one Sun? Yes, it must be, or else He would not say it in the Holy Qur'an! *Rabbul mashāriq wal-maghārib,* "He is the Lord of the Easts (plural) and Lord of the Wests (plural)." There is no end to easts; in every moment He is creating easts. There are infinite numbers of easts and wests! So to accept you, you have to say, *"lā ilāha illa-Hūwa." Awlīyāullāh* order those who are more in seniority, to recite 100 to1,000 times *lā ilaha illa -Hūwa* after *lā ilāha illa-Llāh.* And that is why in *baya*ʿ we recite *Allāhu, Allāhu, Allāhu Ḥaqq,* to enter that ocean of The Unknown.

When He said, *Rabbul mashriq wal-maghrib,* "Lord of the East and the West," what does it mean? Allāh is *Nūr-us-samawāti wal-ʿarḍ,* the rising Sun that shines over everything. That is why we were explained in previous sessions about *shawāriq al-anwār,* when you throw away all these veils and the dust that prevents you from receiving the rising lights. Come to Him with nothing, then you will receive these rising lights and they will manifest in your heart!

Who is The One to Whom all the Lights of all the Names and Attributes are manifested? It is the Prophet ﷺ! He is *Mashriq* (east) and *Maghrib* (west) that is rising all the time and downloading all these Names and Attributes. One of his names is *al-Mashriq* and *al-Maghrib,* because Allāh said, *rabbul mashriq;* that is where all rising lights come from. That is because Allāh is his Lord and that is why He raised Prophet's name with His.

Then what about *rabbul mashriqayn wa rabbul maghribayn?* That has no *sharīk,* no associate to Allāh. He is the Lord of Prophet ﷺ, *Sultan al-Anbīyā* ﷺ, and *Sulṭān al-Awlīyā.* That is the indication of the one who receives directly from the Prophet ﷺ and gives guidance to the *ummah.* And that is also an indication that Allāh gives to the beloved Prophet ﷺ, one who is *Sulṭān al-Awlīyā. Fa bi ayyi ʿalā rabbikuma tukhadhbān,* so who gave you permission to say, no? He is *al-Mashriqayn* and *al-Maghribayn.*

Muḥīyyidīn ibn ʿArabi ق said, "The presence of *Sulṭān al-Awlīyā* is always facing the Prophet ﷺ to receive directly from him." What about the Creator of Easts and Wests? That means He is the Lord of all *awlīyā* that He gave to Prophet ﷺ. They are *shawāriq al-anwār*, spotlights moving in this universe, bringing the kernel of sincerity, *lubb al-ikhlāṣ*. When they carry that sincerity, they become *ayah min ayātullāh*, a sign from Allāh's Signs.

One of Shaykh Sharafuddīn's ق names was *"ayātun min ayātullāh tamshi 'alā al-'arḍ."* When you enter these oceans you find yourself saying, "What I am doing here?" That is why most *awlīyā* are waiting for the day when Allāh calls them to the Divine Presence. When we know that Allāh mentioned Prophet ﷺ as *mashriq* and *maghrib*, as *mashriqayn* and *maghribayn*, and as *mashāriq* and *maghārib*, then we know there is no way to be sincere except through him!

So we have to be always knocking on the door, calling, *"Yā Sayyīdī, yā Rasūlullāh!"* But don't come alone; bring someone with you. If you come alone, they will not open because there is no sincerity in you. You have to bring someone that is accepted, a means, *wasīlah*, vehicle. If you bring your shaykh with you, for sure he has more access than you. When he says, *"As-salāmu 'alayk yā Sayyīdī, yā Rasūlullāh!"* it is different from when we say it. He says it with sincerity, so then they will open the door. For those with no sincerity, they will get rewarded, but the door might not open. You must keep saying it every day and you must not get tired; keep knocking.

"Enter houses through their proper doors." Who are the doors? They are *awlīyāullāh*. Prophet ﷺ said:

Anā madinatu 'l-'ilmi wa 'Aliyyun babuha.
I am the city of knowledge and 'Alī is its door.　　　(al-Ḥakim, Tirmidhī)

Sayyīdinā 'Alī ؏ is the door. In every time, there is an inheritor for Sayyīdinā 'Alī ؏. So come with him and then you see the city. Who did Prophet ﷺ take with him as a companion in his migration? He took Sayyīdinā Abū Bakr aṣ-Ṣiddīq ق. There was never a moment that he was away from Prophet ﷺ. Therefore, he is always inside the city not outside. Inside you will find another door for you to be sure you are in the presence of Prophet ﷺ.

That is why the Naqshbandi Order is called, "the Golden Chain"; it comes from two great humans that are with Prophet ﷺ. Sayyīdinā 'Umar ؏ and Sayyīdinā 'Uthmān ؏ are also among the greatest *Ṣaḥābah* ؏, but they have other assignments, other things to do. The Naqshbandi Ṭarīqah connects these two sources in Sayyīdinā Jafar aṣ-Ṣadiq ق. When we come with these two sources, then Shayṭān becomes exhausted. When that happens, *dunyā* comes to you. But right now, we are slaves to *dunyā.* We are running after work, after *dunyā.*

'Indamā tatajarrad min ṭabi'ati nafsak al-ḥaywānīyya. When you strip from yourselves your animal characteristics and *wujūd al-imkāni,* "the possibilities of your existence," then you can come to *al-wujūd al-jam'i,* "the collective existence" of *awlīyā* and prophets in the Divine Presence. The existence of possibilities has no value. The Divine Existence is a very precious ocean with endless depth. You can dive and dive, and still it is as if you didn't dive at all!

That is why recitation of *"lā ilāha illa-Llāh"* takes you to *wujūd ilāhī,* the Real Existence. If you say, *"lā ilāha illa 'anā,* there is no god except me," which our actions support, that will not take you anywhere; *dunyā* will become your master and you will become a slave to *dunyā.* When you say, *"lā ilāha illa-Llāh",* then *dunyā* will become a slave to you. Say it with sincerity and Allāh will open to your heart.

May Allāh ﷻ forgive us and may Allāh bless us.

Wa min Allāhi 't-tawfiq, bi ḥurmati 'l-ḥabīb, bi ḥurmati 'l-Fātiḥah.
And with Allāh is success. For the sake of the Beloved, for his sake we recite the opening chapter of Holy Qur'an.

Shari`ah Protects the Fruit of Islam, Tasawwuf

Aʿūdhu billāhi min ash-Shayṭān ir-rajīm. Bismillāhi' r-Raḥmāni 'r-Raḥīm. Nawaytu 'l-arbāʿīn, nawaytu 'l-ʿitikāf, nawaytu'l-khalwah, nawaytu 'l-ʿuzlah, nawaytu 'r-riyāḍa, nawaytu 's-sulūk, lillāhi Taʿalā fī hādhā 'l-masjid. Atiʿ ūllāh wa atiʿū 'r-Rasūl wa ūli 'l-amri minkum. (4:59)

O Believers! Followers and students of Mawlana Shaykh Nazim al-Haqqani ق! The Prophet ﷺ said, *kalīmatān khafīfatān ʿalā al-lisān thaqīlatān lir-Raḥmān. Aʿūdhu billāhi min ash-Shayṭān ir-rajīm. Bismillāhi' r-Raḥmāni 'r-Raḥīm.*

As Mawlana Shaykh Nazim ق says, "O our Attenders!" Students of Mawlana Shaykh Nazim ق, we are followers of *Āhlu 'l-Sunnah wa 'l-Jamaʿah*! Therefore, we must behave likewise, not like people with no discipline. Discipline is what leads you to the love of Allāh and of Prophet ﷺ. If Sayyīdinā Muḥammad ﷺ said something, it is to be followed. He left behind his *sunnah,* which is to be followed, to guide us not to be careless about how we behave and act. We have to behave well, and to behave well is to follow the footsteps of Prophet ﷺ. If you follow Prophet ﷺ, you will be happy in this life and the Next.

Prophet ﷺ said, "Don't be like roosters and chickens when you pray, as that prayer is not accepted." He saw someone praying, going quickly up and down, and when that person made *salām*, he told him to repeat his prayer. *Ṭarīqah* is not only *māʿrifatullāh;* although that is important, you cannot leave *dhāhir ash-sharʿah,* the external (practices) of Sharīʿah or then it will be as if you didn't pray. Don't say, "My prayer is accepted, I have a shaykh." No! Your shaykh will not help you when you come against Sharīʿah. Prophet ﷺ said:

> *Kalimatān khafīfatān ʿalā al-lisān thaqīlatān fī 'l-mīzān.*
> *Two words that are very light on the tongue, but very heavy on the Scale.*

There are different *aḥadīth* on that. One of them says, "These words are *SubhānAllāh wa biḥamdihi,*" and according to another *hadīth*, it is the

Shahādah, which Prophet ﷺ said it is to say, *Ash-hadu an lā ilāha illa-Llāh wa ash-hadu anna Muḥammadun Rasūlullāh.*

When you say, "I am *muwwāḥid,*" you have to implement the meaning of *tawḥīd,* which is *sajdah.* That is what Allāh ordered Iblīs to do and he refused. Whether it is a *sajdah* of worship or of respect to the light of Prophet ﷺ in Adam ؑ, when you make *sajdah* you must keep its requirements. What are they? To say, *Subhāna Rabbī al-ʿalā wa biḥamdih,* not to say it like a parrot, (very fast). You have to meditate on it, *al-ʿalā.* The secret of that Name will reach you when you ponder it. "Allāh is High and the rest are slaves to Him!" When you say, *Subhāna Rabbī al-ʿalā wa biḥamdih,* Allāh will dress you with that dress, that *baraka,* when you say it three times in each *sajdah.* Don't allow Shayṭān to exhaust you by pecking the ground like a cock or a chicken.

Who says, *"Subhāna Rabbī al-ʿalā wa biḥamdih"* completely? Some say, *"Subhāna Rabbī al-ʿalā,"* they don't continue saying *"wa biḥamdih."* So when we are not giving all the rights to our prayers, which is a kind of worship that Allāh ordered everyone to do, should we expect we will not have problems? You will have problems in *dunyā* and in *Ākhirah*! What is the benefit of *taṣawwuf* when we are dropping Sharīʿah? We are Muslim first, Shafiʿī or Hanafi (or following another) school of thought. Then we follow a *ṭarīqah,* a Way. So we have to learn Sharīʿah first, and then enter *taṣawwuf.* If we don't know Sharīʿah, we should not attend *taṣawwuf* classes!

Shari`ah Is the Shell that Saves the Fruit

In the previous years, students were not allowed to attend *taṣawwuf* classes at all before being checked in Sharīʿah completely, as it is not simple. In the time of Sayyīdinā ʿAbdul-Khāliq al-Ghujdawāni ق, one of the shaykhs of the Golden Chain, the grand mufti of that time came to him. He said, "*Yā* ʿAbdu 'l-Khāliq, I want to be in that path," because it is the fruit for *ʿulamā.* Sharīʿah is the shell that saves the fruit. They know the importance of the fruit. I remember when all my uncles studied in Azhar ash-Sharīf, you could not graduate except by being in a Sufi Order. Today you can graduate by being an *ʿālim,* but previously you had to have Sharīʿah (law) and *taṣawwuf.*

Imām Malik ق had 300 teachers of Sharīʿah and 600 of *taṣawwuf.* Do you think they taught him to pray like a chicken? We don't understand! Islam accommodates every century, time, culture, and moment in the lives of human beings. We cannot say we have to "Arabinize, Pakistanize, or

Americanize" Islam. Anyone who is saying that is considered *kāfir* (unbeliever)! Did Allāh say that whenever someone comes they can change Islam? No! But He said:

> *Bismillāhi' r-Raḥmāni 'r-Raḥīm, al-yawma akmaltu lakum dīnakum wa atmamtu ʿalaykum niʿmatī wa raḍītum lakumu 'l-Islāmu dīna.*
> *This day I have perfected your religion for you, completed My favor upon you, and have chosen Islām as your religion.* (Sūrat al-Māʾidah, 5:3)

"Today I have perfected and completed," meaning, "There are no additions after I have completed, and I have given you with My satisfaction of my religion." So we can say we want reform Muslims, but we cannot say Islam needs reform; you cannot reform what Allāh made perfect! Muslims are mistaken, not following *sharīʿatullāh,* and not understanding the taste that Allāh gave in His Sharīʿah! When they don't have taste they think, "We have to change Islam," and that is not true. Islam cannot be but what it is. No addition, no subtraction, no multiplication, and no division. Sharīʿah is clear, *al-halālu bayyin wal-ḥarāmu bayyin.* But extremists are doing different things, coming with verses of Holy Qur'an (which they misinterpret). Why blame Islam for the wrong understanding of one person? Blame that person, not the religion!

Imām Malik ق said, *man tafaqaha wa lam yatasawwaf faqad tafasaq,* "The one who studied Sharīʿah without learning the spiritual side will become corrupt." Sharīʿah is the trunk and inside is the *lubb* of the tree. When deer come in the winter and can't find anything to eat, they scrape the bark of the tree and eat the sap. The bark is Sharīʿah and the sap is *taṣawwuf.* So they take Sharīʿah and hold it, then they reach the inside; that means you need both.

That is why he said, "Who studied Sharīʿah and left *taṣawwuf* is corrupt, and whoever studied *taṣawwuf* without Sharīʿah, is a heretic." You cannot be a Sufi and not pray, but you can pray and not be a Sufi. So the first one is, to follow Sharīʿah without *taṣawwuf.* There is no taste; therefore, you are cheating and deceiving, you do what you like. But whoever studied *taṣawwuf* without Sharīʿah is also dangerous as it leads you to be a heretic. Today they say, "We are Sufis." No! You are only hiding behind the name of Sufism, but in reality doing all things that are wrong! Have you seen these big conferences? They speak on *taṣawwuf* and never on Islam.

When we came in 1991 and spoke about *taṣawwuf,* they acted like they never heard of it. How is it possible that Pakistanis, Indians, or Arabs never heard of *taṣawwuf?* Where did you throw *Maqām al-Iḥsān?* There are tons of books by thousands of scholars! Imām Malik ق said that you have to study both the shell and the fruit: the shell saves the fruit, just as the cup saves the water. If there is no cup, there is no water. Where will you put it, in your pocket? No, it will run off and leak. The cup preserves the water.

Lessons from Abdul Khaliq al-Ghujdawani

So the shaykh came to 'Abdul-Khāliq al-Ghujdawāni ق and said, "I want to be your student."

He said, "I have too many students."

The shaykh said, "I have Sharī'ah, but I need to taste the sweetness of the fruit."

It is not like *dunyā* fruits; can you have more than a hundred kinds of fruit? Every moment you will be offered different heavenly fruits with a different taste. And each heavenly fruit is different from the other. So there is an infinite number of different types of fruit. As when Sayyīdinā Zakariyya ४ entered the *mihrab* of Sayyida Maryam ४, he found there provisions of fruit and each time the fruits were new and different. Heavenly fruit never repeats.

The shaykh said, "I don't want knowledge of papers, I want the real taste, *dhawq.*"

So 'Abdul-Khāliq al-Ghujdawāni ق said, "Since you are insisting, I will give you the taste of *taṣawwuf,* some sweet fruit."

The shaykh said, "Yes, that is what I want!" He thought that Sayyīdinā 'Abdul-Khāliq al-Ghujdawāni ق will open a book and explain to him some secrets, because he is an *'ālim* (scholar) and that is how he learned. So he waited and saw the shaykh bringing a donkey, an axe, and a rope.

'Abdul-Khāliq said, "Shaykh al-Islam, you want to learn *taṣawwuf?*"

"Yes, I want to sit with you and learn from you"

He said, "No, you will sit with my donkey!"

People come to Mawlana Shaykh Nazim ق and say, "We want to sit with you." What do you mean? You are nothing; you need to fight with your ego first and then come! These are *sulṭāns;* come to them as such!

So he said, "Go, cut wood, and bring it. That is your job." They were in Merv, where it is very cold in the winter. And he added, "Go up to that mountain and use this road to get there." So how will Shaykh ul-Islam take the donkey up the mountain and bring back wood, as someone might see him. ʿAbdul Khāliq al-Ghujdawāni ق wants to teach him humbleness. "Go and get yourself straightened out."

At one street, people saw him in the village. Children began to throw stones at him. People leave their children, especially in the West. If the children break the whole mosque, it is no problem. Now they made the child the shaykh and adults are their *murīds*! If children are not disciplined in childhood, you cannot later control them when they are older. It is better to give a little bit of discipline when the child is still young, because they will forget you disciplined them. If not, they will grow up and become gangsters and join gangs. How many children around the world are joining gangs? You cannot bring them back.

So the children were running behind him throwing stones, saying, "Shaykh ul-Islam has a donkey!"

He came back and asked ʿAbdul-Khāliq al-Ghujdawāni ق, "Can I change the route and go through the back roads?"

ʿAbdul-Khāliq said, "You want to change something? How dare you even ask me!"

Today Mawlana Shaykh Nazim ق is very soft. He doesn't say anything to people. You should have seen him twenty or thirty years ago! ʿAbdul Khāliq al-Ghujdawāni ق said, "Since you asked, now you have to go through the main roads of the city."

He wants to give him *shawāriq al-anwār,* manifestations of Heavens. One comes, the other goes, and each is different in color. But first, you have to get the key. As Sayyīdinā Mūsā ﷺ objected to Sayyīdinā Khiḍr's ﷺ actions, likewise, Shaykh ul-Islam complained.

At the first level, he said, "Can I go through the road where no one see me?" and ʿAbdul Khāliq al-Ghujdawāni ق said, "No, you go through the main roads now." And as he was going, more children and many people behind him were saying, "Shaykh ul-Islam is crazy."

So he came back, complaining, "O! That original road was better. Can you put me back on that road? They are bothering me on this one too much."

Sayyīdinā ʿAbdul-Khāliq al-Ghujdawāni ق said, "You are saying this, so give me back my donkey, my rope, and my axe. Now go and clean the toilets of the city."

Ṭarīqah is not easy; through it they bring all difficulties to your nose. "Go and clean what people don't." That is why the *khadim* (servant) of the *masjid* is the first to enter Paradise, not the *imām* or the *muʿazzin*. Even if the *imām* memorized the entire Qur'an and *hadīth,* the one cleaning the restrooms will be sent to Paradise first. Allāh looks at sweet people, ones who don't raise their heads, especially who are cleaning the *masjid*; they don't complain that someone asked them to clean the *masjid*. The person who is cleaning is carrying the waste of those who are arrogant. They don't care. They don't say, "We have to volunteer and come to clean the *masjid*." No, they are not caring.

Sayyīdinā ʿAbdul Khāliq al-Ghujdawāni ق said, "You go and clean the city restrooms."

Shaykh ul-Islam knew that he is not giving difficulty to him, but to his ego. So he did as the shaykh said. Forty days later, he came back and the shaykh said, "Now you can receive your trust." Sayyīdinā ʿAbdul Khāliq al-Ghujdawāni gave him his *amānah*.

So Sharīʿah is first, but you have to combine it with *ṭarīqah*. Or else, you will feel arrogant. Therefore, you need to say, "*Yā Rabbī,* I don't know and they don't know. Whatever you inspire to my heart, that is what I need and they need." May Allāh keep us on the track of Ahl as-sunnah wal-Jamaʿah, or else we will be falling on the ways of Shayṭān and never coming out.

Today, unfortunately we are falling into this problem; we don't accept advice. If someone tells you something, don't say, "Who are you?" Listen, you may benefit. When Shaykh Sharafuddīn ق was asked, "Why are you giving so much attention to that young one (Grandshaykh ʿAbdAllāh)," he said, "My nephew? If a child now will go to his house and say, 'Your shaykh is telling you to go to Madinah or to Mecca,' he will not *yatarajā*, hesitate. Without any doubt and without asking anything, without even saying farewell to his wife and children, he will open the door and start walking to Mecca or Madinah. He will not question or say, 'I need a ticket or a camel or a donkey, or provisions.' He will go forward, not backward!"

Not even say *salām* to his wife. Who can do that now? *Taṣawwuf* is belief in what the shaykh says, or you believe, "When someone says something to me I do it, knowing my shaykh might be making that person speak."

May Allāh ﷻ forgive us and may Allāh ﷻ bless us.

Wa min Allāhi 't-tawfiq, bi ḥurmati 'l-ḥabīb, bi ḥurmati 'l-Fātiḥah.
And with Allāh is success. For the sake of the Beloved, for his sake we recite the opening chapter of Holy Qur'an.

Awliyaullah Teach Tawhid by Example

A'ūdhu billāhi min ash-Shayṭān ir-rajīm. Bismillāhi' r-Raḥmāni 'r-Raḥīm. Nawaytu 'l-arbā'īn, nawaytu 'l-'itikāf, nawaytu'l-khalwah, nawaytu 'l-'uzlah, nawaytu 'r-riyāḍa, nawaytu 's-sulūk, lillāhi Ta'alā fī hādhā 'l-masjid. Atī' ūllāh wa atī'ū 'r-Rasūl wa ūli 'l-amri minkum. (4:59)

A*llāhu Akbar*! This small instrument (smart phone) has a picture of a microphone, and the phone is recording everything; taking pictures, recording sound, and storing it for whenever you need it. This is a *dunyā* innovation. Allāh's Creation is more and more advanced. Why is there competition? Allāh's Creation is much more able to take this knowledge and store it, and whenever we need it we can access it. Allāh ﷻ cannot leave his servant in the hands of Shayṭān, so He gave us ammunition and said, "Use it." How should we use it? By performing *'ibādah.*

Allāh said in Holy Qur'an:

Ma khalaqta al-jinna wa 'l-ins illa li-ya'budūn. mā urīdu minhum min rizqin wa mā urīdu an yuṭ'imūn.

And I created not the jinns and ins (humans) except they should worship Me (Alone). I seek not any provision from them, nor do I ask that they should feed Me. (Sūrat adh-Dhāriyāt, 51:57)

There might be a lot of *jinn* sitting here; if we can see, we see them. "I didn't create *jinn* and *ins* except to worship Me." This means there are *jinn* among us, sitting and listening. I don't know if they are sitting now and listening, but for sure *mu'min jinn* will sit and listen wherever Allāh's Name is mentioned. So what does Allāh want from them? Worship. He didn't create them to work. "I don't want any *rizq* from them, to provide themselves. I will provide for them." But people today are greedy, they want too much. So Allāh ﷻ is saying, "Okay, if you want too much, struggle for it. I gave some people too much because it is My will and no one can object. To some people I gave a little bit; that is My will and no one can object."

It is said that Allāh ﷻ has given His *awlīyā* their needs, without them running or struggling, as they struggled enough on Allāh's Way, and now Allāh gives to them for the benefit of His servants, to help them. One duty is *ash-shukr,* to thank Him. *Awlīyā* are thanking him, and we are forgetting. We thank Him when someone recovers from a sickness; then you say, "*Yā Rabbī*, thank you!" Then you remember. (An attendee entering the assembly stumbles.) Just now Allāh gave an immediate sign to confirm what we are saying: someone tripped. Allāh doesn't want anything from us. He wants us to remember Him, *bi shukri tadūm an-niʿam,* by thanking Him, His provisions continue to you.

Awliya Are Generous

Awlīyāullāh's provision is endless. They offer a tray for ten to fifteen people and they all eat with their hands. In past times, all shared the same tray, not like today where everyone has a plate and we are wasting money. There was one plate for ten to fifteen people and everyone takes his share. That plate has endless *barakah* given to *awlīyāullāh's* food. They never run out. They are thanking for the food in front of them and Allāh keeps giving without you seeing.

For some of them, Allāh puts the *barakah* in the food, so that food increases more and more. That is a sign of the *aqṭāb awlīyā,* (a *quṭb*): *Budalā, Nujabā, Nuqabā, Awtād,* and *Akhyār. Some people come to them needing* money; for some Allāh sends angels, by His Wish, angels, that put like this under that *walī's* prayer rug whatever they need. When he doesn't have, he puts his hand under his prayer rug, takes from there and gives to others.

Did you see that in your life, someone taking money from under his carpet and give it? That is rare; it is only for certain *awlīyā*. I saw it. Once in Damascus in the eighties, there was someone who had to pay money to an official institution to repay a government loan and it was very crucial or he would go to jail. It was a big amount of money. I witnessed that. So he collected that money and put it in a bag, it was over one million, and they don't deal with checks there so he was carrying cash. He was on his way to pay, when there was an airstrike on Damascus. That car was blown up, the money was gone, but that person was safe! All that money burned and disappeared, but the government didn't care and told him, "You still have to pay!"

Where could he go to get the money? He had heard that on the mountain there is someone who is a *walī,* so he went to him. He drove up the mountain with three or four Mercedes Benz sedans, and his security detail, going up the mountain to that *walī's* house. People were running from all over the mountain to see that. They had never seen black cars with dark tinted glass and security. They all wondered, who are these people

That man got out of the car to see the *walī*. These are from *karamāt* al-Awlīyā. He stepped down and went down directly to that tiny house that was standing just through *barakah;* it may be if you shake one of its wooden pillars the house will go into *sajdah*! He came in, and that *walī* welcomed him. He came and sat there and didn't talk.

Then he said, "O my shaykh! Pray for me."

That *walī* said, "I was praying for you before you came here, you don't recall that you were saved? I was there."

Immediately he kissed the shaykh's hand. That person was from Āhlu 'l-Bayt and was very well-known. There was war in the streets. I was sitting there.

He said, "*Yā Sayyīdī*! I am in a big problem; I have to deliver that money to that institution, and it's gone. I need your help." He looked at the shaykh and said, "At least I can postpone that payment until you can help me. I am ready to take this one down with me to speak with the officials to tell them the money is coming!" And he looked at *me*!

I said, "How we can go during all this bombardment?"

He answered, "Don't worry, I can bring a military tank here to take you down to speak with them."

That *walī* said, "No need. We have people to speak to. Come tomorrow."

I said to that *walī (*Mawlana Shaykh Nazim), "You are promising him, but where will you get that money?"

He said, as usual, "Don't worry: *mā 'urīdu minhum min rizqin wa mā 'urīdu 'an yuṭʿimūn.* "I seek not any provision from them nor do I ask that they should feed Me. (I only want them to worship Me.)" (51:57)

What! Not to worry? That was thirty years ago and it is like today, still people worry too much. I was at that time in my early thirties. These people to whom he had to give the money are not normal people, they are mafia types, very dangerous. So he came the next day and brought lots of food in cooking pots, maybe forty trays of rice and meat, brought on something like a truck. Mawlana called the whole district to come and eat. All lined up and came to eat that food that, with Mawlana's *barakah*, never finished. They ate and prayed Dhuhr, then ʿAṣr, and then they wanted to go. Mawlana put his hand under his carpet and brought out a piece of paper. I looked. That man was shocked.

He said, "These people need cash!"

Mawlana said, "Take this piece of paper and don't talk, don't tell me anything, just take it and go!"

Sometimes Mawlana is very serious, so the man took the paper. I was very curious to see what was on the paper. Written on it, like a check, "Take this paper and deposit it." And usually they never accept paper to deposit. But the man took the paper and deposited it. The next day he came and kissed Mawlana's feet and said, "O Mawlana! They took the paper." Even though they never accept checks, and in three or four days that money was in that man's account! You cannot imagine that, but I saw it.

And *awlīyā* provide for Āhlu 'l-Bayt; so many poor homes of Āhlu 'l-Bayt are living from that one's generosity. *Awlīyā* don't turn away the Āhlu 'l-Bayt; they help them and that is a miracle and *wa khalaqAllāhu ʿalā sajādatihi aw khalwatihi darāhim.* "Those who are on Allāh's Way, Allāh will not put them down." He will create under their carpets money to help the needy!

So we have to learn, for *dunyā,* if you want a lot of money, struggle. No problem; work hard and get it, but if you want a normal life you don't need to struggle because Allāh ﷻ will make *dunyā* a slave for you. Today anyone who goes to visit Mawlana Shaykh will never leave without something in his hand, and Mawlana is sitting on his couch and not working. He just goes and opens the drawer and the drawer is always full. You didn't see the drawer where he is sitting? Where is the drawer? Near his feet, anyone could come, open it and take. Allāh ﷻ provides for them as they provide for the *ummah.*

You Cannot Take the Fruit without the Shell

Now those people want the fruit, they don't want only the shell. Sharīʿah (law), *Ḥaqīqat* (reality), *dhahir* (remembrance), and *bāṭin* (the hidden) are important for them. They have to go side by side, parallel to each other. You cannot take one and leave the other or the scale is not in balance.

Sayyīdinā ʿAbdul Qadir Jilani said, "*ʿIsma kalāmī*!" They are strong and not playing with their *murīds.* If you have sincerity in your heart, and what is on your tongue is also what you show in your actions—not that what you show on your tongue is not what you have in your heart, not if they are something else—that sincerity will *yudfiʿ nāru ṭabaʿk*, put out the fire of your ego. The ego has been raised since childhood. The *walī* has been raised, Allāh made his father and mother raise him in a straight way, and they have pure parents who raise their children well. It depends on how you raise your child, as you reflect on him good or bad characteristics.

That is why we say, *an nafs at-tiflatil-madhmūmah,* "the spoiled-child ego." That is called *tabaʿ*, "imprinted character" from mother and father and the environment around you. So if the environment is *Shayṭānic* then what will come? It is the same for the child. So if your environment is sincere, it will put out the fire of your *nafs* and break the arrogance of your self, that you think you are so important that you don't want anyone to say anything to you.

But you should know that if someone says bad things to you, if they curse you and you keep quiet, you get rewards. If you don't keep quiet and you lose your temper, then you are fighting back and you lose the reward. So don't show your anger, that will break your arrogance and your temper will come down. That anger comes with arrogance. And you don't go to a place if you know there will be a fight; if you go to involve yourself, you are losing. If you let your feet take you to a place where there is a problem, you are destroying the house of your religion.

Nafs, dunyā, hawā', Shayṭān: these are the four things destroying your religion. *Nafs*, the self, and *dunyā,* the world; the head of every sin is love of the world and Shayṭān is pushing you to go there. They take your religion and your world. Don't listen to those *munafiqīn,* hypocrites, who are fake and decorate themselves with all kinds of importance. Because *at-tabaʿ*, the self, has grown on the kind of characteristic that always like to listen to *kalām muzakhkhraf*, ornamented, fancy words.

That is why, and I am sorry to say, scholars have fancy words in their presentations. As you go in to their talks, you come out the same (without benefit), because there is no *barakah.* They are not *awlīyā* and they cannot dress you in what they are speaking. *Awlīyā* have very simple language.

Like Ibn Muqafa ﷺ, who used a language called *as-sahil al-muntaniʿ*, "the easy language," but no one else can do it. *Mumtaniʿ* means, "difficult." He was most famous for that. It is very simple language, but very hard to imitate. *Awlīyā* have that kind of language, that is so simple, but it goes to the heart.

Their language is so simple but so strong. Scholars cannot do that. They describe to you, but Allāh didn't give them the authority to dress you with what they are saying. Some give you fancy words but cannot dress you with what they say, and others speak very simply but can dress you with the realities. Fancy words are like dough that has not been cooked well and has no salt (taste); it is still raw and when you eat it your stomach becomes upset. When you sit in the presence of these scholars, you feel okay as they are making the dough, but when you go out you have darkness coming on you, because their words have arrogance. You can be a scholar but know your limits, and when you stand at the door of a *walī* you must respect what the *walī* says.

During his *ṣuḥbah* Mawlana said to someone, "*Sayyid*, come," and it is rare that Mawlana stops his *ṣuḥbah*. It means, "Come and sit near me," as that one was sitting on the floor. That was Habīb ʿAlī Jafri, who said, "O my shaykh! Give me *ijāzah* on *dhikr*." That means, "Give me a *wird* to use for *barakah*."

That is how they show they know the level of *awlīyā*, and in what relationship they stand. So he knows this one, although Mawlana speaks a simple language, and they respect it because they are real *ʿulamā*, and he showed respect to Mawlana. If you show respect to *awlīyā*, Allāh gives you more. From that visit ʿAlī Jafri is going to be higher, as he humbled himself to visit Mawlana.

The Shaykh Bakes Your Ego

So the difference is, when *awlīyā* make the dough it is cooked well and there are no upset stomachs. When they put the dough in the fire, know that the shaykh is cooking your dough, your ego. He has to cook it very well and sometimes he might burn it because it is too much and not a normal dough that will be fixed with heat. He has to burn your ego completely so you can receive. When your ego is finished then you can see all these manifestations. And *awlīyāullāh* know when you are ready.

Once we were coming to Grandshaykh's house, where you have to go through a narrow alley about two meters wide, and on one side is the house and on the other side is the mosque, and you pass under the window. As we were passing under it, we heard Grandshaykh ق shouting and shouting and shouting. That was in 1969; time is passing. We were mesmerized and could not move, because if he sensed our presence we may have entered that problem, that fire! We didn't know who was in there. Grandshaykh was shouting all kinds of words, I will not repeat them now. And at the end he said, "Go! I don't want to see you here!"

From his house you leave through an alley, and we saw Mawlana Shaykh Nazim coming out, smiling!

We said, "Mawlana! How can we go up, already you had a shower."

He said, "Go up."

So you go up the stairway and then in the hallway, and the door for Grandshaykh's room is there, and we heard him shouting for us by name, "Come, come, come." We thought, "O no! He saw us," not with normal sight, but he knew. Me and my brother, Shaykh Adnan, entered there trembling, and Grandshaykh ق looked at us, smiling.

He said, "That Nazim Effendi, however much I shout at him, his love never changes. I was shouting at him by order of Prophet ﷺ and I never saw in him any change, in his eyes or in his face."

Awlīyā are happy with that. We knew that was not a test, but a sign that you are put in a situation that he shouts at you to know how much you are progressing. Then he offered us tea and began a big *ṣuḥbah*. His *ṣuḥbah* is not for forty minutes, it is hours long, depending on how much *tajallī* is coming. *Awlīyāullāh* know you, and know the ego, and attack it to take away anger!

Today Mawlana cannot speak to any *murīd* like that, because they will not come back if he shouts at them. You must be careful and be happy when he shouts at you, as he is lifting away your sicknesses! When a doctor says you have an infection, *Yā Allāh*, they inject you with antibiotics at a dose more than the level of infection, to eat it. Similarly, *awlīyā* are eating your ego and *sayyi'at* when they shout at you, so be happy! Then they are taking responsibility and liability for you, and they will be asked in front of Prophet ﷺ, then you are free.

At that time, Grandshaykh ق said to us, "Don't put me in a position of shame in front of Prophet, when I present you in *sajdah* after Ṣalāt an-Najāt."

That is their responsibility and the reason Allāh gave them sainthood. May Allāh keep us under their wings to be saved in *dunyā* and *Ākhirah.*

Ash-Shādhilī ؓ, *imām* of the Shādhilī Order, said, *"At-tawḥīd sīrrullāh,* that Divine Oneness is the secret of Allāh's knowledge, *was-sidqu sayfullāh,* and by saying the truth and being trustworthy you become Allāh's sword. *Wa madadu sayfī bismillāh,* and the support of this sword is by *Bismillāhi' r-Raḥmāni 'r-Raḥīm."* That sword will be moving and we will discuss this tomorrow.

You see, look outside and take *ḥikmah,* wisdom. It is seven o'clock and still dark, but yesterday it was seven o'clock and sunny. What happened? Today the clouds hide the Sun, but the Sun is there. So the heart is a Sun on which Allāh manifests His Beauty, on the hearts of human beings, but if there is cloud you cannot see, it is dark. So Shayṭān tries to put veils. *Awlīyā* say there are 70,000 veils between us and Prophet ﷺ. You need a shaykh to burn them. So sometimes they let you do something in order to shout at you, and that works out nicely (as when they shout, they lift the bad character that veils you). So that cloud is covering the sun of your heart. If we do not make sure Shayṭān is not taking over our hearts then the veils becomes very thick, like in Antarctica, where it is snowing and snowing, and for thousands of years ice has been building up into an iceberg or "ice shelf" that doesn't melt.

Today they sell dry ice, which doesn't melt easily and lasts longer. Regarding the ice of the heart, the *Shayṭānic* veils on the heart are so thick, it becomes so difficult to dissolve them. As doctors today use lasers to take a stone from the bladder, your shaykh is your laser and he can shoot those thick veils and, *Allāhu Akbar,* what happens? It dissolves them completely. That is what we need, a "laser shaykh," not a "flashlight shaykh." (laughter) He shoots his laser and destroys the veils completely and immediately. It disseminates, takes the knots away completely and shows you your reality.

These meetings under Mawlana Shaykh's name are taking away the veils like a laser treatment, but leaving the common veil, *hijab al-awām.* It is very thick, and they keep it until you are ready for them to take it away. May Allāh take away our veils, so that we see the reality of our shaykh and the reality of Prophet ﷺ!

May Allāh ﷻ forgive us and may Allāh ﷻ bless us.

Wa min Allāhi 't-tawfiq, bi ḥurmati 'l-ḥabīb, bi ḥurmati 'l-Fātiḥah.
And with Allāh is success. For the sake of the Beloved, for his sake we recite the opening chapter of Holy Qur'an.

The Secret of the Name "Allah"

A'ūdhu billāhi min ash-Shayṭān ir-rajīm. Bismillāhi' r-Raḥmāni 'r-Raḥīm. Nawaytu 'l-arbā'īn, nawaytu 'l-'itikāf, nawaytu'l-khalwah, nawaytu 'l-'uzlah, nawaytu 'r-riyāḍa, nawaytu 's-sulūk, lillāhi Ta'alā fī hādhā 'l-masjid. Ati' ūllāh wa ati'ū 'r-Rasūl wa ūli 'l-amri minkum. (4:59)

Whatever we have spoken about this month on issues of *dhikrūllāh* and the best characters, it is the description of how *awlīyāullāh* lived their lives through *dhikrūllāh* and *Maqām al-Iḥsān*. They are not like regular people; they live in a regular life, but Allāh gave something special to their hearts, as the Prophet ﷺ said, "Allāh has given to Abū Bakr aṣ-Ṣiddīq, *shay'in waqara fī qalbihi,"* something that took root in his heart, beyond description. The *Ṣaḥābah* ؓ were wondering about that and later they knew it was *dhikrūllāh*. He was always remembering Allāh ﷻ on his tongue and in his heart.

Once the Prophet ﷺ made his famous *ḥadīth, Allāhummā lā takilnī ila nafsī ṭarfata 'aynun wa lā aqal,* "O Allāh! Don't leave me to my ego for the blink of an eye or less." The eye blinks twenty to thirty times per minute, maybe more. Prophet ﷺ said, "O Allāh! Don't leave me to myself for the blink of an eye." He wants to express in that in such a short moment, two or three seconds, "If I rely on my ego I might fall down."

The Seal of Messengers ﷺ is *ma'ṣūm*, infallible, and he is saying, "O Allāh! Don't leave me to myself for the blink of an eye or less." What is less? How much less? It might be a lot less. He knew, since Allāh ﷻ gave him knowledge that in a fraction of a second, time disappears. Scientists recently discovered that if you go 10^{-22} of a second, it becomes energy only and time disappears. It means, "O Allāh! Don't ever leave me to myself."

What about us? When he heard this *ḥadīth,* look how Sayyīdinā Abū Bakr aṣ-Ṣiddīq reacted. It is completely different than what we do. For us, we hear hundreds of thousands of *ḥadīth*. So what will we have? We never change. Can a donkey be changed? Its ears are always long; it might be we are donkeys with long ears. We never change; we hear, we hear, we hear, and it is the same, *ṭaba'*, as what you have been raised on. That is your photocopy, your print. We are a photocopy of ourselves. However we were raised from childhood, that is what we are. So don't spoil your children from childhood. Don't give them what they like, but give them what they don't like. Today everyone gives their children what they like. Just now we were speaking and we jumped up out of anger. This is our character, all of us.

So immediately, Sayyīdinā Abū Bakr aṣ-Ṣiddīq ؓ jumped up and disappeared. He went and took a stone and put it in his mouth, and went inside the Ka'aba and wept. They were looking for him but not finding him, and Prophet ﷺ knew where he was.

He found him and said, "O, where were you? For seven days you did not come."

Abū Bakr was crying and Prophet ﷺ put his hand between his shoulders and calmed him down, like when Allāh ﷻ made the fire of Sayyīdinā 'Ibrāhīm ؑ to be a cool breeze, around 69 degrees Fahrenheit, and he was very happy inside that boiling fire. When the Prophet ﷺ put his hand on Abū Bakr, all the fire that was in his heart from crying was extinguished.

Prophet ﷺ said, "Why are you crying?"

He said, "Yā Rasūlullāh! I know you are the Seal of Messengers and Allāh gave you shafā'a to intercede for believers on the Day of Judgment. You are infallible, and still you said, 'O my Lord! Don't leave me to my self for the blink of an eye.' What then will happen to me, if I leave myself to my ego for the blink of an eye?" Two seconds. Count it. It is so quick! How many times does Shayṭān come to our heart in a second or less?

Sayyīdinā Muḥammad ﷺ said, "Yā Abū Bakr! Allāh mentioned you in Holy Qur'an two times, when He said:

Illa tanṣu Rūḥu faqad naṣarahu 'Llāh. Idh akhrajahu 'Lladhīna kafarū thānīya ithnayni idh humā fī 'lghār. idh yaqūlu li-ṣāḥibhi lā taḥzan inna 'Llāha ma'nā fa-anzal 'Llāhu sakīnatahu 'alayhi wa ayyadahu bi-junūdin lam tarawhā wa ja'ala kalimat 'Lladhīna kafarū as-suflā wa kalimatu'Llāhi hīya 'l-'ulyā wa'Llāhu 'Azīzun Ḥakīm.

If you help him not, still Allāh helped him when those who disbelieve drove him forth, the second of two; when they two were in the cave, when he said to his comrade, "Grieve not. Lo! Allāh is with us." Then Allāh caused His Peace of Reassurance to descend upon him and supported him with hosts you cannot see, and made the word of those who disbelieved the lowest, while Allāh's Word became the highest. Allāh is Mighty, Wise.

(Sūrat at-Tawbah, 9:40)

He is "the second of two." He and the Prophet ﷺ were together in Ghāri Thawr, when they emigrated from Mecca to Madinah. "He made you my friend. No one took that honor but you." Sayyīdinā Abū Bakr ؓ was older than Prophet ﷺ. "And He called you aṣ-Ṣiddīq al-Akbar, 'the greatest *ṣiddīq*.' Whatever I said, you would say, 'It is the truth, *yā Rasūlullāh*.' He made you *Ṣādiq* and *ṣiddīq*."

Sayyīdinā Abū Bakr ؓ said, "*Yā Rasūlullāh*! On Judgment Day, if Allāh calls me and says, 'I made you *ṣiddīq* and I made you *Ṣādiq* and I made you second in the cave,' and then He says, 'Now I am changing it,' can anyone object or complain? No. So whatever He said about me, on Judgment Day He can change it. Then what will happen?" That also means, "*Yā Rasūlullāh*! Allāh gave you *shafāʿa* but if He changes it, He changes it."

That will never happen, as Allāh will never change His grant! But Prophet ﷺ heard this and began to cry with him. Grandshaykh ق always told this story to let us know that if Allāh will change something, then what will happen? We will be in a gray area with our *ʿamal,* and for sure we will go to Hellfire, but with Allāh's mercy we are in Paradise! So they were both crying, and there were rivers of tears coming from their eyes. Why did they cry? Each tear that came from the eye of Prophet ﷺ represents a human being, and the Prophet cried on all human beings of *Ummat an-Nabī* until Sayyīdinā Jibrīl came and said, "Stop!"

Those individual drops represent one human being, and all of them are under the *shafāʿa* of Prophet! Allāh said it in Holy Qur'an:

> *Walladhīna maʿahu ashiddāu ʿalā al-kuffāri ruḥamā'u baynahum.*
> *Muḥammad is the Messenger of Allāh, and those who are with him are severe against disbelievers, and merciful among themselves.* (Sūrat al-Fatḥ, 48:29)

Here *kuffār* may mean "the self." You cannot be loose on your ego and tough on others; you must be loose on others and strict on your ego! And Allāh gave the same for the People of the Book, those believing in the Injīl (New Testament), and those believing in the Torah of Mūsā (Old Testament).

Naqshbandiyya Are Created from Sayyidina Abu Bakr's Tears

So Sayyīdinā Abū Bakr ؓ was crying and crying, and by Allāh's order he stopped. When he cried, each tear that fell represents one Naqshbandi follower, and each will be under safety! Then Sayyīdinā Jibrīl ؑ came and said, "Allāh sends His *salām* and says, 'As much as my Lordship, I am not changing! They have a certificate of *bara'ah,* innocence." Do we have something like that? If so, be happy and keep smiling and laughing all your life! If not, we have to remain worried about what will happen to us. So it is not only reading; we read hundreds of *ḥadīth,* and what changed in us? Nothing.

Treatment from 'Men Who Reached Manhood' (Sainthood)

How can you change? If you are sick, if your body is infected, you take injection of antibiotics, or you take pills or whatever there is, and the only remedy is an injection from outside you; it is not coming from within you. You cannot swallow tablets without putting your hand on your tongue. You cannot have an injection with holding your hands together. That injection has to come from outside, then it has an effect, but if from inside it has no effect.

Sometimes they give not only antibiotics, but anti-inflammatories and Cortisone, if the illness is severe. So who can prescribe what you need? You need a doctor. So Sayyīdinā Abdul Qadir al-Jilani said, *'ālim yukhadh min afwāhir-rijāl lā min aṣ-ṣuḥuf.* That injection has to "come from the mouth of men who reached manhood (sainthood)." Also ladies reached sainthood; we cannot say no.) So anyone who reached the level of sainthood is able to diagnose your sickness and prescribe what you need, an injection that has to come from outside you, not from within you.

That is why he said, *al-'ilm yukhadh min afwāhir-rijāl lā min aṣ-ṣuḥuf,* "It cannot be taken from papers, it has to be taken from their mouth or their eyes, and they send on you *'Ilmu 'l-Yaqīn* (Knowledge of Certainty), *'Aynu 'l-Yaqīn* (Eye of Certainty), and *Ḥaqqu 'l-Yaqīn* (Reality of Certainty). They give you an injection that gives you knowledge and raises you up, first to the level of *'ilm,* knowledge, then to the level of *'ayn,* vision. With another deadly injection, they raise you to the level of *ḥaqq,* the reality, where there is no more question about *tawḥīd.* Your understanding is certain, in your heart and mind, then you know that everything in this life points to the Creator. There is no more hesitation or doubts, finished! That has many levels, which we might discuss in the future.

So he said, don't take from papers. *Awlīyā* can use papers to teach you, but they have to sit with you, diagnose you, and prescribe the unique medicine for you. That is why they came through the *awrād.* The different *ṭarīqahs* have different *awrād,* each shaykh has his way and they might not intersect. Each *ṭarīqah* has its own *awrād* and techniques. In the Naqshbandi Way we have to follow from shaykh to shaykh, and in the *silsilah,* chain, the *awrād* may change; as time changes, they may change.

I mentioned many times that Grandshaykh ق never gave *baya*ʿ to anyone and now Mawlana Shaykh gives everyone *baya*ʿ, even on the phone or through the Internet! It depends on the time. So don't take from papers, but take it from mouth of *awlīyā,* as they will guide us.

Who are these "men"? *man hā ulai'-rijāl.* Sayyīdinā Abdul Qadir al-Jilani ق is telling his students in the famous work, *al-Faid ar-Rabbani,* "They are the men of truth; *al-muttaqūn,* they are sincere, they have *taqwā; at-tārikūn,* those who left *dunyā,* they let it down; *al-wārithūn,* inheritors of the Prophet; *al-ʿarifūn, man ʿarafa nafsahu faqad ʿaraf rabbah,* those who reached level of knowing Allāh; *al-mukhlisūn,* the sincere ones; *mukhlis,* who are straight on the Straight Path; *al-ʿāmilūn,* never changing from what Allāh made them to be (not like us, sometimes Mawlana says something and we don't act on it); *rijālun sadaqū mā 'aḥad Allāhu ʿalayh,* men who are true to their promise, they never changed.

We change all the time, *lā ḥawla wa lā quwatta illa billāhi 'l-ʿAlīyyi 'l-ʿAẓīm*! We are changing every time and getting older and getting worse! Sayyīdinā Abū Yazīd ق said, "I respect the elder and I respect the younger. The young have less sins and the older has more worship." Now it is rare to find someone of the same age in a city; with globalization you find many people born at the same time.

So choose: men who kept their promises with Allāh, *wa mā badalū tabdīla,* they never changed throughout their lives and they are waiting for the time they will go to Allāh; whatever they are on, they are on. Are we changing? (Yes.)

Sayyīdinā Abdul Qadir ق continues, "And whatever else we have described is *hawwas* (hallucination) and *bātil* (false)." It is obsession: you want something, you need it and you don't want to let it go. You don't want to let *dunyā* to go. Who wants *dunyā* to go? No one. You want *dunyā,* then you are obsessed by *dunyā;* when you are obsessed by *dunyā* that is *bātil.* So what he said? *al-wilāyatu li 'l-muttaqīn,* "If it is not obsession and it is true, then it is right." *Muttaqīn* means "God-fearing," those who are conscious of their Lord. So those who keep their promises are those to whom Allāh ﷻ gave *dunyā* and *Ākhirah.*

Allāh said, *Rabbanā ātinā fi 'd-dunyā ḥasānatan wa fi 'l-ākhirati ḥasanat,* to ask good in this life and Next. That is first level of being a true one, then you go higher and you want *Ākhirah* only, then you go higher and you want only Allāh ﷻ. There are people who dropped *dunyā* completely, even non-Muslims, monks in shrines. What will Allāh do with them? We leave that judgment to Allāh. There are people who left *dunyā* and they want to be truthful to what they believe. We have to keep our truth to them in order to be saved. *Allāhummā ṣalli ʿalā Muḥammad*! That is why he said, *abʿad nafsaka ʿani 'sh-shubuhāt, wa 'sh-shahawāt,* "Don't go near gray areas from bad desires," *aʿwadh nafsaka ʿalā akal al-ḥalāl* "and make your ego to eat from what is *ḥalāl.*"

Sayyīdinā Abdul Qadir al-Jilani ق is not speaking of meat; it means, "eat from your sweat, work!" Allāh doesn't like people who are lazy. Are you working? (No, I lost my job.) Okay, I have a job for you. Go to the *masjid* and clean the toilets. Don't sit at home like a chicken; show *ʿamal* and work! Like in Europe, they grant government aid to those who have children and no work. So what are they doing? They are becoming manufacturers of children; they reproduce child after child and take money! That is a business, keeping themselves busy and not lazy! (laughter)

(A baby cries.) That baby is confirming what we said. Don't be lazy, waiting for a job to open! Show Allāh that you are working, even by selling something at cost (without profit). Show Allāh that you want to eat from your sweat! Otherwise, do *ʿibādah*. Do something instead of sitting all day watching TV, eating steaks and hamburger!

W 'aḥfaẓ bāṭinaka bi 'l-murāqabah, "Protect your inner self by doing *murāqabah.*" Don't say meditation doesn't exist: Ghawth al-ʿAdham, ʿAbd al-Qādir al-Jilānī ق is mentioning it! Keep *bāṭin,* your inner self, working. If you have no work, then place a sheet over your head and for eight hours, as you normally work eight hours, do eight hours of meditation and *ʿibādah* in addition to the worship you must do. Then make an account of what you did; that is for the inside, that no one sees (internal worship).

For the outside (external) that you can see, follow the *sunnah* of the Prophet ﷺ, who said, "If you love Allāh, follow me (my *sunnah*), then Allāh will love you." If Allāh loves you, you will be lucky. Then you get correct inspirations: you will hear and see. Don't say, " I am in *ṭarīqah* 25 years and not seeing anything." You reached a limit and if you break through it, then it will open for you. Don't want the shaykh to break it for you! They want you to break it, because then you will go up very high, but if shaykh breaks it you only stop at that level. So you have only one chance in life to break it.

Take that chance! Then you will have right inspiration and it will hit right on target.

At that time you will be granted *mari'fatullāh*, allowed to reach heavenly divinely knowledge. May Allāh guide us! That is why Imām Shādhilī ☙ said, *at-tawḥīd sirullāh*, "(To make *dhikr* by *tawḥīd*) *lā ilāha illa-Llāh* is the Secret of Allāh." *Qul Hūw Allāhu 'Āḥad*, "Say, 'He is the One Who is unique and He is known by the Name "Allāh".'" That concept is the Secret of Allāh! *wa 'ṣ-ṣidqu sayfullāh*, "To say the truth is the sword of Allāh," to fight the ego, not to go and fight and blow up people. Kill your self, the ego, first! And the support for the sword is by reciting, *Bismillāhi' r-Raḥmāni 'r-Raḥīm*.

May Allāh bless us and support us, and give our shaykh long life to see Sayyīdinā Mahdī ☙ and Sayyīdinā 'Īsā ☙, and give us long life!

Wa min Allāhi 't-tawfīq, bi ḥurmati 'l-ḥabīb, bi ḥurmati 'l-Fātiḥah.
And with Allāh is success. For the sake of the Beloved, for his sake we recite the opening chapter of Holy Qur'an.

Characters, Powers & Responsibilities of the Ghawth & His Aqtab

A'ūdhu billāhi min ash-Shayṭān ir-rajīm. Bismillāhi' r-Raḥmāni 'r-Raḥīm.
Nawaytu 'l-arbā'īn, nawaytu 'l-'itikāf, nawaytu'l-khalwah, nawaytu 'l-'uzlah,
nawaytu 'r-riyāḍa, nawaytu 's-sulūk, lillāhi Ta'alā fī hādhā 'l-masjid.
Ati' ūllāh wa ati'ū 'r-Rasūl wa ūli 'l-amri minkum. (4:59)

A*wlīyāullāh*, as we have described through these 29 days or less, have different levels and knowledges they carry in their lives. They have a strong willpower and never stop until they reach their goal and then they continue more. And it is said:

Awliyāī tahta qibābī lā ya'lamahum ghayrī.
My awlīyā are under My domes; no one knows them except Me.
(*Ḥadīth Qudsī*)

Which saints are not known? Allāh knows them, and He knows how much they have achieved and rewarded! And we described through different sessions about their levels and what they have done. There is the *ghawth,* and under him the five *quṭbs:* Quṭb, Quṭb al-Bilād, Quṭb al-Aqtāb, Quṭb al-Irshād, Quṭb al-Mutaṣarrif. And under them are five different *awlīyā*: *Budalā, Nujabā, Nuqabā, Awtād,* and *Akhyār*. All are taking from Prophet ﷺ through their connection and their lineage, and we have mentioned that. The only one we have not described is the *ghawth.*

He takes from heart of Prophet ﷺ directly and he is *fardu 'l-jamī' al-wāḥid,* he is the unique one to whom Allāh ﷻ gave the power of keeping all *awlīyā* together. Everything goes back from him to Prophet ﷺ. He is the one that Allāh looks at seventy thousand times daily and sends on him manifestations of His Beautiful Names and Attributes, and daily these manifestations change. The *ghawth* is the one about whom Allāh ﷻ said:

Mā wasi'anī arḍī wa lā arḍī wa lākin wasi'anī qalbi 'abdī al-mu'min.
Neither Earth nor Heavens contained Me, but the heart of the believer contained Me.

The *ghawth* can carry *an-Nūr al-Ilāhī*, the Heavenly Light Allāh sends. He can carry all the rest of the ummah and whatever they receive depends on their level, if they can pull it or not. He has four other sides to know: one, he takes from the heart of and carries the secret from (archangel) Sayyīdinā Azrā'īl ☽, who is described as *"amadat ul-ikhsas."* Allāh gave him a specialty from the "material of life and feelings," which is the secret Allāh put in every Creation to appear. The appearance is in the heart of Sayyīdinā Isrāfīl ☽ (Archangel Rafael). When he blows the trumpet, He will pull life out from every Creation and they will die. Then another time he will blow the trumpet and give them that sensation of the reality of life, and they will come back.

The *ghawth* takes from that knowledge, and he also takes from Sayyīdinā Jibrīl ☽ (Archangel Gabriel), the secret of "the talking self," the ability of talking through *nashāṭun insānīyyah*. It begins when the child or creature begins talking in his own language that Allāh gave him. Human beings have a language they all know, one universal language through which Allāh ﷻ made everyone communicate.

That language is in the reality of Sayyīdinā Jibrīl ☽, because he was the one who revealed the message to all prophets in one language that all of them understood. What he gave to Sayyīdinā Adam ☽ was in the same language as what he gave to Sayyīdinā Ibrāhīm ☽, Sayyīdinā Nūḥ ☽, Sayyīdinā Mūsā ☽, Sayyīdinā 'Īsā ☽, and Sayyīdinā Muḥammad ﷺ! It is the language that the heart understands and all human beings know it.

A contemporary example is, you have many languages in technology, but all can communicate in the same language. So that is the language the heart understands, but it is veiled. The *ghawth* carries that reality.

Then he takes from Sayyīdinā Mikā'īl ☽ (Archangel Michael), because Allāh gave him power to shower rain on human beings.

Wa ja'alna mina 'l-ma'ī kulla shay'in ḥayy.
We have made from water every living thing. (Sūrat al- Anbīyā, 21:30)

•

Life may come through that. The *ghawth* knows that secret of life from the heart of Sayyīdinā Mikā'īl☽; he takes from that and moves them. And then he takes from Sayyīdinā Isrāfīl ☽ the power of taking people from life to death; he has the power to bring back people as Allāh wishes. He is always looking when Allāh will order him to go and take the souls of people. It means that *ghawth* takes the bad characters from people and gives them good characters on their hearts without you knowing he is doing that, by the secret that Sayyīdinā Azrā'īl ﷺ is carrying in his heart. These are the specific functions of *al-ghawthīyyatu 'l-kubra,* the greatest *quṭbīyyah,* also known as *ghawthīya quṭbīyyah.*

The Ghawth Gives Heavenly Support

Ghawth means "*yughīth,*" who gives *madad,* support. He is carrying from these four angels and taking from the heart of Sayyīdinā Muḥammad ﷺ. He is the one who is able to take whatever he needs for his job, and that is not a normal job, it is a heavenly reality that has been thrown in the heart of that *ghawth.* And he has *lahu imāman,* two *imāms* or two helpers, one on the right, one on the left.

The one on the right is always looking at what is needed to get from heavenly powers, and he is the center of receiving heavenly and spiritual support. And the one who is on his left looks at all Creation and supports them with heavenly sources directly. He is responsible for everything that Allāh created, to send to them power so they will be feeling their existence on Earth. If that *walī* pulls out, everything will faint and fall down; there will be no power!

These two *imāms* have eight characteristics: four are *ẓāhir* (apparent) and four are *bāṭin* (hidden). The apparent characteristics are: they are *az-zuhhād,* ascetics; they are *dhu 'l-war'a,* always active in doing good things and doing what Allāh ﷻ likes; *al-amr bi 'l-m'arūf wa 'n-nahīyy 'ani 'l-munkar,* they call people for good, and prohibit them from doing wrong. But their hidden knowledge, that they don't reveal, is *aṣ-ṣidq,* they keep their covenant with Allāh ﷻ, and they don't change, they stay on their promise. They have *ikhlāṣ,* sincerity, *ḥayā,* shyness, and they are always in *murāqaba,* meditation.

The *'abdāl* are under them. They are *hum Āhlu 'l-faḍl wa 'l-kamāl,* "people of honor and perfection." *W 'astiqāma wa 'l-'itidāl,* they stay on the right path and are always in the middle, on moderation, not too much on the right or the left. Allāh took removed imagination and doubt from them. They are the ones mentioned by Prophet ﷺ in his holy *ḥadīth:*

> *If you are in a desert or a jungle and you are feeling fear, call on rijālAllāh; they will come to you and support you.*

Al-Budala and al-Nujaba

Then there are *"al-Budalā."* It is said they range in number from 40 to 300. Then are *"al-Nujabā,"* they are from 40 to 70 in number. *Budalā* support people in their fears or difficulties, and grant things to them in *dunyā* matters, while *Nujabā* do things for their *Ākhirah* matters. Their work is to carry all the heaviness of bad character, *asqal al-ʿibād,* the burdens of people. They don't look anywhere except at the Divine Presence, through the five *quṭbs,* to the *ghawth,* and then to Prophet ﷺ. Their orders come from there directly, and that is what Muḥammad al-Busayrī ق knew.

He described the realities of these *awlīyā* as, *wa kullum min rasūlullāhi multamisun,* "Everyone is taking from Prophet ﷺ, asking for support and *madad."* They are well known for *kathrat al-ʿibādah,* they are always in worship. And they are always in *muhasaba* and *wa tafakkur,* analyzing the accounts of human beings; if low, they recite *ṣalawāt* and give that to the human being.

That is why human being's level rise up, and instead of remaining negative it becomes positive. If they see someone falling down on the negative side, they push them to the positive side. It is their job to keep everyone on the positive side and they don't allow anyone to go negative.

One of their characters is *at-tafakkur,* they remain in concentration. They do not give an ear to this *dunyā.* They are always perfect.

The Nuqaba

Then are the *Nuqabā.* Allāh ﷻ gave them a different power, that they are able to reach human beings without saying anything. They keep quiet, they don't talk except through their hearts. That is why *awlīyāullāh* have one or two hours in meditation, because the strength of the heart is more than the strength of the tongue. They are very well known for *aṣ-ṣamt,* silence, and to keep awake at nights *as-sahr,* and *al-juʿ* and they are always hungry, as Prophet ﷺ said:

> *Naḥnu qawman lā nākul ḥattā najuʿ, wa idhā akalnā lā nashbʿa.*
> *We are people who don't eat until we are hungry, and we don't eat until we are full.*

Nuqabā remain hungry and their stomachs are always grumbling; that keeps them awake. They are in complete *ʿuzlah,* they seclude themselves.

They have their own *imām* who leads them to the presence of Prophet ﷺ. They are *qad tahaqaqu bi 'ism al-bātin*, certain about what is hidden, and *ashrafu bi bāṭin an-nās*, able to observe what is hidden in people, and *fastakhrajū kashaif ad-damāir*, they extract the hidden aspects of the subconscious mind. For them all veils are taken away.

Today we see that with psychiatrists; you begin to speak to them and they ask you questions and through your answers they analyze your problems. *Nuqabā* don't need that as they go directly to the subconscious and to the heart, and pull that out of the heart. So to pull all that from people, the psychiatrists need psychiatrists! So don't go to psychiatrists, go to *Nuqabā*. With Allāh's support, they know what is hidden and by that the people are cured, as *Nuqabā* are not veiled and can see.

The hidden aspects of the subconscious have three characteristics. First is *an-nufūs al-'alīyya fa hiya haqāiqul-amrīyya*, the highest level of the subconscious; when you are in a good way, you establish that high level in the subconscious and that is the certainty and reality of heavenly orders. Their eyes are on that, as it is highest level and they will come to heavenly orders.

In each day there are 24 hours and all information of what will happen is written in the Preserved Tablets. Whatever you have to do is written there, and they can see that. For everyone else that is veiled, but for them it is not veiled and they pass it to you. Then you can get this information to your heart, or your shaykh keeps it for you. That is *nufūs al-'aliyya.*

The second characteristic is *nufūsun suflīyya*, the subconscious that is connected with evil, it is the lowest of realities. First is positive and second is connected to Iblīs and Shayṭān, and all that is connected to the subconscious, the inner lower conscious where all these bad gossips come to the heart. The third characteristic is *nufūs al-wa satīyya*, the reality of human nature. It is in the middle level. In all the three levels, Allāh ﷻ has put a chip or implanted there all heavenly secrets that concern that person.

These heavenly secrets are 360. Why 360 secrets? Because in the body there are 360 points that you can press and activate, and every point has its secret and every point on human beings or creatures has a pressure button to activate a certain language to know what is needed in 24 hours. So these *awlīyā* are able to get that information and if you are on the right path with your *awrād*, then this information is sent to you by *awlīyā*. Then, if your power is strong, the power of these points is sent to you as inspiration.

If you are not on the right path, then *nafs as-suflīyya* will be activated, giving you bad information. If you drop both of them, then you activate *an-nafs al-ʿulwiyya;* that higher self that is always there in presence of Prophet ﷺ, in the Divine Presence. If you are able to connect to all three, these veils will be taken; if you are unable, then *Nuqabā* will bring these matters to you.

Al-Awtad and Akhyar

Al-awtād are not too many: they are four in the east, four in the west, four in the south, and four in the north. *Awtād* are like tent pegs that stabilize the tent, which has four sides, so you have four stakes. *Awtād* are the stakes of this world, the poles that keep everything strong in the east and west, north and south. They are responsible for every group in those four regions.

Allāh gave them eight different actions they must do. The apparent actions are *kathratus-siyām,* they fast excessively; *qiyam ul-layli wan-nāsu niyam,* they are awake all night and always vigilant of what is going to happen; *wa kathratul-imtithal,* they are always submitting and they say, *samiʿna wa ataʿna,* "We hear and we obey," and they never say, "no" or use their minds, and whatever is sent to them, they accept; and the fourth apparent action is, they are always in *istighfār* when people are sleeping.

That is what we can see from them. What we cannot see are their hidden actions: *hum al-mutawakilūn ʿalā Allāh,* they always put their trust in and depend on Allāh and Prophet ﷺ, they have strong trust, *thiqah;* and they are always in *taslīmiyya,* perfect submission. Then there are many of their characters we have described in these lectures.

Al-Akhyār are the last type of *aqṭāb,* and are those who have been honored, picked up, and selected. Not everyone can be from that group and it is very limited. *Akhyār* are directly under the five *quṭbs* and they are *akmal ahl al-arḍ,* "the most perfect of the people of Earth."

You see no difference from their physical appearance and their hidden appearance; they have balanced them. You see them as normal people. They don't have beads in their hands (to indicate piety). They go here and there, and people say they are not *awlīyā,* so why are they going there? They go for a certain reason, which you don't know. They act normally, but they are the most perfect of the people of Earth.

They never let the right hand to know what left is doing and they never put in their hearts to do any bad action or take revenge; they have no bad intent and always take everything with good intent. They know you are

Allāh's servant and they cannot criticize Allāh's servants, they have to cover them. Their arteries are saturated with the taste of sincerity. They have no other taste, but the taste of sincerity throughout their physical and spiritual bodies.

They have love to everyone and no criticism. They don't like anyone to know about them. They move through the *ummah* wearing what normal people wear, they don't say, "We need a *jubba*;" they wear normal clothes. Physically and spiritually they look like us, so trust them! They look normal, if they look different then you not will know them.

Grandshaykh ق said, "These type of *awlīyā* are there every 24 hours. Even if someone is living by himself on the peak of a mountain with no humans around, in every 24-hour period there must be one of these *awlīyā* visiting him or passing by, because they give their support to everyone. These are the ones who appear. Allāh gave them the ability to appear to every person physically, or spiritually through dreams."

This is the conclusion of "Ramadan Series 2010". May Allāh ﷻ grant Shaykh Nazim al-Haqqani long life and good health, and may Allāh bless us to be with him, to see Sayyīdinā Mahdī ؑ!

Wa min Allāhi 't-tawfiq, bi ḥurmati 'l-ḥabīb, bi ḥurmati 'l-Fātiḥah.
And with Allāh is success. For the sake of the Beloved, for his sake we recite the opening chapter of Holy Qur'an.

One Holy Gathering Will Erase a Million Sins

A'ūdhu billāhi min ash-Shayṭān ir-rajīm. Bismillāhi' r-Raḥmāni 'r-Raḥīm.
Nawaytu 'l-arbā'īn, nawaytu 'l-'itikāf, nawaytu'l-khalwah, nawaytu 'l-'uzlah,
nawaytu 'r-riyāḍa, nawaytu 's-sulūk, lillāhi Ta'alā fī hādhā 'l-masjid.
Ati' ūllāh wa ati'ū 'r-Rasūl wa ūli 'l-amri minkum. (4:59)

This is an important reminder for us all. When you want to pray, what do you do before prayer? You make *wudu* to clean yourself from anything that might affect your prayer from sins that you have done before praying. We cannot say that everyone is perfect and does not do any mistake or a sin between one prayer and another prayer. And also if you want to read Holy Qur'an you need to be clean, and Allāh ﷻ ordered us in Holy Qur'an:

> *Fa idhā qarāt al-Qur'an fasta`idh billāhi min ash-Shayṭān ir-rajīm. Innahu laysa lahu sultānun `alā alladhīna amanū wa `alā rabbihim yatawakalūn.*
> *Now whenever you read this Qur'an, seek refuge with Allāh from Shayṭān, the Accursed. Behold, he has no power over those who have attained faith and who in their Sustainer place their trust.* (Surat an-Nahl, 16:98-9)

Listen well, you and me. Allāh is saying, "When you want to read the Holy Qur'an, then seek refuge in Allāh from Shayṭān. He has no power over those who have *taqwa* and those who are *mu'min*, he cannot come to them, and *tawakkalū*, trust in Allāh." That means whenever you want to do an action, say, *"A'ūdhu billāhi min ash-Shayṭān ir-rajīm. Bismillāhi' r-Raḥmāni 'r-Raḥīm."* You are saying, "I am seeking refuge in Allāh ﷻ and in His Name I am beginning this action." So it is going to be a successful action or a failing action? Of course it is going to be successful, because Allāh said that.

So every `*amal* has its door and the door of every `*amal* is (to say), *"A'ūdhu billāhi min ash-Shayṭān ir-rajīm. Bismillāhi' r-Raḥmāni 'r-Raḥīm."* When you sleep, you say, *"A'ūdhu billāhi min ash-Shayṭān ir-rajīm. Bismillāhi' r-Raḥmāni 'r-Raḥīm. Ash-hadu an lā ilāha illa-Llāh wa ash-hadu anna Muḥammadu 'r-Rasūlullāh."* The last word before you sleep has to be *Shahādah*. If someone died in his sleep, then his last word was *Kalīmatu 'sh-Shahādah*. You don't sleep without saying the *Shahādah*, so you sleep saying,

"*Aʿūdhu billāhi min ash-Shayṭān ir-rajīm.* I am seeking refuge in Allāh ﷻ and I am saying, *'Bismillāhi' r-Raḥmāni 'r-Raḥīm,'* in His Name I am beginning the action of sleeping." You are now *bayna yadayyi Raḥmān,* between Allāh's Hands, and you don't know if you will wake up or not.

It is also recommended to sleep with *wudu.* Now some people might have *wudu* and some people might not, but it is best to have *wudu* because when you recite that, Allāh ﷻ will take the soul under *`Arsh* to make *sajda.* When you wake up, open your eyes saying, "*Aʿūdhu billāhi min ash-Shayṭān ir-rajīm. Bismillāhi' r-Raḥmāni 'r-Raḥīm. Ash-hādu an lā ilāha illa-Llāh wa ash-hādu anna Muḥammadu 'r-Rasūlullāh.*" When you begin your day this way, Allāh ﷻ will not let:

> *Kullu `amalim lam yabdā bismillahi fa huwa abtar.*
> *The Prophet ﷺ said, "Any action which does not begin with 'Bismillāhi' r-Raḥmāni 'r-Raḥīm' is cut off; it has no continuity."* (Ahmad, *al-Musnad*)

Every *`amal* that does not begin with *'Bismillāhi' r-Raḥmāni 'r-Raḥīm'* is cut off, with no benefit. Do you need benefit in *dunya* and *Ākhirah*? Then mention "*Bismillāhi' r-Raḥmāni 'r-Raḥīm*" there.

So why are such associations like these meetings so beneficial; why are we coming to these meetings? Are we coming by ourselves or is there someone pushing us to come? There is a push, we are being pushed. If you want to go by yourself, you will never try to come to such meetings and there are many other places that you can enjoy. Here all of us are coming and listening, and here anyone can speak, but we listen because our coming here is for Allāh and His Prophet ﷺ.

There are two ways: either association for Allāh and His Prophet or association for *dunya*. The one for *dunya* is supported by Shayṭān and the one for *Ākhirah* is supported by *Raḥmān,* so it's up to us to choose which way we want. So do we have sins? Yes, we do. How to erase them, how to take them away? In how many associations do we sit for *dunya,* speaking nonsense and might be making sins, watching TV and doing all kinds of things that Allāh and His Prophet ﷺ does not like? We are not saying that you are perfect or we are perfect. No, you will fall, you will do that, but what is important is that you need a cleansing process. This association is a cleansing process and look how much Allāh ﷻ has given you from attending such associations of *dhikrullāh,* what you will get, and when you attend associations with no *dhikrullāh* what you get. Any association that doesn't have *dhikrullāh,* which is only for *dunya*, to play for Shayṭān, I am sorry to say that all of us have this problem and it will be written that you committed one sin, two sins, three sins, ten sins from an association that you went to.

For example, in a place where people meet, you will see all kinds of different sins: the way people are acting, the way people are dressing and behaving there. You took yourself to such an association, so it is going to be written that you committed a sin in one association. Allāh writes *hasanah* ten times, but He will write a sin one time. So such associations for *dunya* are going to be written as a sin. Now it can be written five, ten, one-hundred or two-hundred sins. Allāh will not over write more than what you deserve; if what you deserve is five, ten, one-hundred or two hundred sins, that is what will be written, but look for the associations of attending *dhikrullāh,* like these association, what you will be given.

The Power of Attending a Gathering of Dhikrullah Even Once

Prophet ﷺ said, as narrated by Imam Ahmad in his *Musnad*: *Al-majlisu 's-ṣāliḥu yukaffiru `ani 'l-mu'min alfayya alfa majlisīn min majālisa 's-sūw.* "*Al-majlisu 's-ṣāliḥ*" is the pious gathering, like this gathering. People are leaving everything worldly and coming here, but what are they gathering for? For a good gathering, to benefit. Even if they are not doing anything, only sitting and remembering Allāh ﷻ in silence, still they are written in *majlisu 's-ṣāliḥ*, a pious gathering, which takes away *yukaffiru `ani 'l-mu'min,* all sins from the shoulders of a *mu'min* and erases from his life the sins of one-thousand multiplied by one-thousand (1000 x 1000) bad gatherings! One good association like this association, if we did it once in our life, will take away from us one-thousand times one-thousand bad gatherings in which we sat in *dunya,* which means one-million bad gatherings!

How can you reach one-million bad gatherings? Even if you commit sins of bad gatherings and you live for one-hundred years, if you multiply that by 365 days that would be 36,500 days that you will live. If every day you had a bad gathering, one good gathering will erase the 36,500 and the balance will be written for you as good gatherings, because it erases one-million and no one can do one-million! So Allāh is saying to you, "Sit for Me in one good gathering and I will erase from you one-million bad gatherings!" So this is a reward that Allāh gives for those who are sitting and benefiting, but benefitting how? What are they remembering? They are remembering the good manners and the good behaviors, sitting together nicely and happily, remembering each other and remembering things you did in the past in such gatherings.

Also, it is said by Prophet ﷺ and narrated by Imam Ahmad:

Inna ahla 'dh-dhikri la-yajlisūna ilā dhikrillāhi ta`ala wa inna `alayhim min al-āthām mithla 'l-jibāl wa ghanahum la-yaqūmūna min dhākiran-Llāhu mā `alayhim minhā shayy.

The Prophet ﷺ said that people sit in good gatherings, like *dhikrullāh* gatherings, they remember Allāh ﷻ, and on their shoulders they have mountains of sins. With this gathering, *la-yaqūmūna min dhakara-Llāhu mā `alayhim minhā shayy,* "They walk out from this gathering clean, all their sins having been erased." Those two hadiths are enough for us to understand how much Allāh ﷻ is rewarding His Servants for a small *`amal* and by this small *`amal,* it will erase big and bad *`amals.*

Do you know yourself? No.

Man `arafa nafsahu faqad `arafa Rabbah.
Who knows his self knows his Lord.

When you know yourself and know that you need such gatherings, then you know Allāh ﷻ wants you to go to such gatherings. You might find them in *masājid,* you might find them in homes, you might find them anywhere, only if you look for them. But what do we look for? Bad gatherings. We want to be with bad people. What did the Prophet ﷺ say?

Allāhumma ahyinī miskīnā wa amitnī miskīnā wa 'h-shurnī fi zumrati 'l-masākīn.
O Allāh! Make mine a miskīn (needful) life and let me die miskīn and resurrect me in the gathering of the miskīn.

This is the Seal of Messengers ﷺ, the one about whom as human beings we cannot fully speak about or describe as that is impossible. Only Allāh describes His Prophet ﷺ, no one else! Sometimes out of respect and love to Prophet ﷺ, we put his sandal on our *jubba* or on top of our turban. All of that, *alhamdulillah* you are doing it and it is okay, but no one can praise the Prophet ﷺ except Allāh ﷻ. Look at what the Prophet ﷺ said. This is the taste of Islam and if we don't or cannot feel it, if it is dry, and true religion is not dry, if you go to places where you are only hearing, "Don't do this, don't do that! You are going to Hell, you are going to Hell!" then people will go in either two ways: either they become extreme or they become depressed and they don't know what to do.

If you have a tyrant ruler, you immediately become depressed and you don't know what to do as you are under a tyrant's oppression, but if your leader is not a tyrant, if he is merciful with you, you run to him. So what do you think about the Creator of this universe, Who is The Most Merciful, The Absolute Merciful?

Wa raḥmātī wasi`at kulla shayin fasa'aktubuhā lilladhīna yattaqūna wa yu'tūna 'z-zakāta wa 'Lladhīnahum bi ayātina yu'minūn.
My Mercy encompasses everything. That (mercy) I shall ordain for those who do right and practice regular charity, and those who believe in Our Signs.
(Surat al-`Arāf, 7:156)

"My Mercy has encompassed everything and I will write it for those who are *mu'min*, I will dress them with it," which means, "I will dress those who come to such gatherings."

And look what the Prophet ﷺ is saying. "O Allāh! *Ahyinī miskīnā,*" meaning, "When you give me life, give me life as a *miskīn.*" *Miskīn* is a person who is in need, he is needy, but here, as scholars have explained it, it is humbleness: to be *miskīn* is to be humble. The humble one is always *miskīn* and you always see him *miskīn* because he humbled himself. You look at him and say, "*SubhānAllāh*! This one is pure, he is humble, *miskīn.*" "Miskīn" also means he has nothing of *dunya.*

"Raise Me with the Needy"

So the Prophet ﷺ said, "*Yā Rabbī*! Create me as *miskīn* in this *dunya,* I don't want to own anything from it. *Wa tawaffanī miskīnā,* and take my soul *miskīn,* take my soul when I have nothing, *Yā Rabbī*! Don't give me, I don't want *dunya. Wa 'h-shurnī fi zumrati 'l-masākīn,* and resurrect me with the group of *miskīn.*"

That is what the Prophet ﷺ is saying. What about us? We always want the top, we have to be recognized. Don't you see them when you are in an official meeting and some official leaders are there, they say, "O! We recognize Mr. Senator so-and-so, we recognize Mr. MP so-and-so." Recognize them for what? Put yourself under the dirt, under the soil, like what Sayyidina `Umar ؓ said, "If my *`amal* tomorrow is not better than today, then it is better for me to be underground than to be above ground! If my *`amal* is better tomorrow than today, then I am okay, but if it is not...." It means he wants to be improving all the time. Are we improving all the time? No, we are eating each other, we are biting each other like wild animals! At least domestic animals do not bite you. Sometimes a horse or a donkey may kick you, but wild animals will eat you! "O Allāh! Create me *miskīn*," means, "*Yā Rabbī*! Create me not interested in *dunya*." That is why the Prophet ﷺ said:

Innamā bu`ithtu li utammimu makārim al-akhlāq.

I have been sent to perfect the best of conduct (your behavior and character). (Bazzār)

That is because Allāh ﷻ taught him that, and He perfected him:

Adabanī rabbī fa'ahsana tā'dībī.

My Lord perfected my good manners and conduct.

(The Prophet is saying,) "Allāh ﷻ has disciplined me and perfected my manners and I want to reflect this perfection on the *ummah*." Don't think that you can do anything without the support of Prophet ﷺ in *dunya* and in *Ākhirah*! Every moment of your life needs the support of the Prophet ﷺ and we have to learn:

Wa law kunta fazhan ghalīzh al-qalbi la-anfadū min hawlik. Fa`fuw `anhum wa astaghfir lahum wa shāwwirhum fi 'l-amr.

And had you been severe and harsh-hearted, they would have broken away from about you; so pass over (their faults) and ask (Allāh's) Forgiveness for them, and consult them in the affairs. (Surat Āli-`Imrān 3:159)

Allāh ﷻ is saying, "(*Yā Muḥammad*!) If you were *fazh,* rigid, vulgar, harsh and *ghalīzh al-qalbi,* a tough, heavy-hearted person, what would happen? Everyone would run away from you." Allāh is saying to the Prophet ﷺ in the Holy Qur'an, *wa law kunta fazhan ghalīzh al-qalbi la-anfadū min hawlik,* "If you were," but he is not, so Allāh says *wa law kunta,* "If you had been, people would run away from you." Instead, people are running towards the Prophet ﷺ!

The example is those who don't have sins are running toward the Prophet ﷺ! Who does not have sins? Angels have no sins and they are running toward the Prophet ﷺ, making *ṣalawāt* on him because he is pure.

Wa law in kunta fazha ghalītha al-qalbi la anfadū min hawlik, "They would have run away from you, but they did not."

When the Prophet ﷺ was on a journey passing through mountains and deserts, he said he was hearing the *taṣbīh* of mountains and the animals speaking to him. If he was not humble and soft, they would have run away. Even wild animals came to the Prophet ﷺ and we are wild animals in our characters; every person has a wild characters in him. Allāh ﷻ said, "If you were rude to people and had a heavy heart, then people would run away." Why do people like to run after all of you here? Because you have that humbleness.

So for that reason, Prophet ﷺ said:

Awsā 'n-nabiyyu sall-Allāhu `alayhi wa sallim Aba Hurayrah bi-wasīyyati `azhīmatin fa-qāla: Yā Aba Hurayrah raḍiAllāhu `anhu, `alayka bi-husnu 'l-khuluq. Qāla Abu Hurayrah: wa mā hasana 'l-khulqi Yā Rasūlullāh. Qāla: tasila man qata`k, wa ta`fū `amman zhalamak, wa tu`tī man haramak.

(Narrated by Bayhaqi)

"*Yā* Abu Hurayrah!" Prophet ﷺ is mentioning to Abu Hurayrah ؓ, who is one of the biggest *muhaddith*, confirming and affirming to him, *`alayka bi husnu'l-khuluq,* "You have to carry the good manners, the good characters in you, you have to be good, your personality has to carry good manners."

Abu Hurayrah ؓ said, *man ahsana 'l-khulqi Yā Rasūlullāh,* "What is the best of characters, *Yā Rasūlullāh*?"

Now I am asking you: what is the best of characters that is always among people? We have something in common, all of us. What is that? It is a character that if you get upset with someone, you cut your relationship with him, is it not? What is the Prophet ﷺ saying first? *An tasila man qata`k,* "To reconnect with someone who cut you off." If you have a problem with him or he has a problem with you, one of you has to find a way to reconnect with each other. So the Prophet ﷺ said, *an tasila man qata`k,* you are ordered to reconnect with the one who cut you off (not the one who cut you off has to reconnect with you). You have to go to him and bring him back to connect with you by asking his or her forgiveness, although you did not do anything, they disconnected from you and cut you off.

Islamically, from standards of good manners as the Prophet ﷺ described, you are the one to come first. If anyone cut you off, you have to go to him and say, "Please forgive me if I did something wrong, let's restore our relationship."

Then? *Ta`fū `amman zhalamak,* "And to forgive the one who oppressed you, harmed you." How many people have harmed you? Too many, too many! But what is the order from the Prophet ﷺ? *An ta`fū `amman zhalamak,* "To forgive those who harmed you." Don't say, "They harmed me," but forgive them for Allāh's Sake. You forgive more and they beat you up more, as Allāh ﷻ is testing your patience: are you going to surrender or not?

How much was the Prophet ﷺ harmed? He said, "Not one prophet was harmed as much as my tribe and family harmed me!" yet he was always extending his hand!

So first, "*an tasila man qata`k,*" second, "*ta`fū `amman zhalamak.*" First, to connect with the one who cuts you off, second, to forgive the one who harmed you, and third, *tu`tī man haramak,* "To return blessings for harm." (For example,) I own property with you. What did you do? You forged my signature and ran away with the property, then you sold it and put the money in your pocket. What must I do? If you come to me for help, even after all that still I have to help you! This is what the Prophet ﷺ is saying: *an tu`tī man haramak,* "To give something to the one who prohibited you from what you were supposed to get."

Allāhu Akbar! Who can do that? Especially between families you see that a lot, between brothers and sisters: they cut each other from inheritance and they take everything. What did the Prophet ﷺ say? Let them take everything, give them more and tell them, "Take! If you are hungry, I am giving to you more. I want to see where it ends with you." *Shajā` wa 't-tama`a,* greediness and *shajā`*, horrible characters. *Shajā`* is too much greediness and *tama`a* is greediness. So if you do that, you will be safe.

So what is the advice?

Yā Waladī! O my son! *Usīkum an tajtanib bal aqdāl wa ahli 'l-fasād wa 'd-dalāl.* So then what you need to do now? If you are unable to fix these, to do what Prophet ﷺ mentioned of the good manners, the best is to avoid making friendship with bad people, to pull yourself out; don't meet with them because they will reflect their bad characters on you, because everyone reflects his bad energy on you. You have good energy, because such good associations give good energy, but if you go out you associate yourself with bad people and they give you bad energy. That's why when you go out to malls, supermarkets and so on, lots of bad energy is flying around and you will be affected.

May Allāh bless us and support us, and give our shaykh long life to see Sayyīdinā Mahdī ﷺ and Sayyīdinā ʿĪsā ﷺ, and give us long life!

Wa min Allāhi 't-tawfiq, bi ḥurmati 'l-ḥabīb, bi ḥurmati 'l-Fātiḥah.
And with Allāh is success. For the sake of the Beloved, for his sake we recite the opening chapter of Holy Qur'an.

Islamic Calendar and Holy Days

The Islamic calendar is lunar-based, with twelve months of 29 or 30 days. A lunar year is shorter than a solar year, so Muslim holy days cycle back in the Gregorian (Western) calendar. This is how Ramaḍān is celebrated at different times of the year, as the annual Islamic calendar is ten days shorter than the Gregorian calendar.

Four Islamic months are sacred: Muharram, Rajab, Dhūl-Qʿadah and Dhūl-Hijjah. Holy months include "God's Month" (Rajab), "Prophet's Month" (Shaʿbān) and the "Month of the People" (Ramaḍān), in which pious acts are rewarded more generously.

Months of the Islamic Calendar

1. Muḥarram
2. Safar
3. Rabīʿ ul-Awwal (Rabīʿ I)
4. Rabīʿ uth-Thāni (Rabīʿ II)
5. Jumāda al-Awwal (Jumādi I)
6. Jumāda uth-Thāni (Jumādi II)
7. Rajab
8. Shaʿbān
9. Ramaḍān
10. Shawwāl
11. Dhū'l-Qʿadah
12. Dhū'l-Hijjah

al-Hijra

The 1st of Muharram marks the beginning of the Islamic New Year, chosen because it is the anniversary of Prophet Muḥammad's ﷺ historic *Hijra* (migration) from Mecca to Madinah, where he established the first, preeminent Muslim community in which he introduced unprecedented social reforms, including civil law, human and women's rights, religious tolerance, taxation to serve the community and military ethics.

ʿAshura

On 10th Muharram, ʿAshūra commemorates many sacred events, such as Noah's ark coming to rest, the birth of Abraham, and the building of the Kaʿbah in Mecca. ʿAshūra is a major holy day, marked with two days of fasting, on the $9^{th}/10^{th}$ or on $10^{th}/11^{th}$ based on a holy tradition (*ḥadīth*) of Sayyīdinā Muḥammad ﷺ.

Mawlid

Mawlid al-Nabī, 12th Rabiʿ al-Awwal, commemorates Prophet Muḥammad's birth in 570. Mawlid is celebrated globally throughout this month in huge communal gatherings in which a famous poem "Qasīdah al-Burdah" is recited, accompanied by drummers, illustrious poetry recitals, religious singing, eloquent sermons, gift giving, feasts, and feeding the poor. Most Muslim nations observe Mawlid as a national holiday.

Laylat al-Isra wal-Mi'raj

Literally, "the Night Journey and Ascension;" 27th of Rajab is when Sayyīdinā Muḥammad ﷺ physically traveled from Mecca to Jerusalem, ascended in all the levels of Heaven from a rock in the Dome of the Rock, and returned to Mecca—while his bed was still warm. In the Night Journey, Islam's five daily prayers were ordained by God. Sayyīdinā Muḥammad ﷺ also prayed with Abraham, Moses, and Jesus in Jerusalem's al-Aqsa Mosque, signifying that Muslims, Christians, and Jews follow one god. This holy event designated Jerusalem as the third holiest site in Islam, after Mecca and Madinah.

Laylat al-Bara'ah

The "Night of Freedom from Fire" occurs on 15th Shaʿbān. On this night God's Mercy is great; hence, the night is spent reciting Holy Qurʿan and special prayers, as well as visiting the deceased.

Ramadan

Many regard Ramaḍān, the ninth month of the Islamic calendar, the holiest month of the year. Muslims observe a strict fast and participate in pious activities such as charitable giving and peace making. It is a time of intense spiritual renewal for those who observe it. Fasting is meant to instill social awareness of the needy, and to promote gratitude for God's endless favors. The fast is typically broken in a communal setting, and hence Ramaḍān is a highly social month. At night, a special Ramaḍān prayer known as "*Tarawīh*" is offered in congregation, in which one-thirtieth of the Holy Qurʿan is recited by the *imām* (prayer leader); thus the entire holy book of six thousand verses is recited in this month.

Eid al-Fitr

"Festival of Fast-Breaking" marks the end of Ramaḍān and is celebrated the first three days of Shawwāl. It is a time for charity and celebration with family and friends for completing a month of blessings and joy. In the Last Days of Ramaḍān, each Muslim family gives "Zakāt al-Fitr"(charity of fast-breaking) which consists of cash and/or food, to help the poor. On the first early morning of Eid, Muslims observe a special congregational prayer, such as Christmas/Easter Mass or the High Holy Days. After Eid prayer is a time to visit family and friends, and give gifts and money (especially to children). Many specialty foods and sweets are prepared solely for Eid days. In most Muslim countries, the entire three days of Eid is a national holiday.

Yawm al-Arafat

"Day of 'Arafat," 9 Dhul-Hijjah, occurs just before the celebration of Eid al-Adha. Pilgrims on Hajj assemble for the "standing" on the plain of 'Arafat, located outside Mecca, where they contemplate the Day of Standing (Resurrection Day). Muslims elsewhere in the world fast this day, and gather at a local mosque for prayers. Thus, those who cannot perform Hajj that year still honor the sacrifice of Abraham.

Eid al-Adha

The "Feast of Sacrifice," celebrated from the 10th-13th Dhul-Hijjah, marks Prophet Abraham's willingness to sacrifice his son Ismā'īl on God's order. To honor this event, Muslims perform Hajj, the pilgrimage to Mecca that is incumbent on every mature Muslim once in their life if they have the means. Celebrations begin with an animal sacrifice to commemorate Sayyīdinā Abraham's sacrifice. In Islam, he is known as *Khalilullāh*, "God's friend." Many consider him the first Muslim and a premiere role model, for his obedience to God and willingness to sacrifice his only child without even questioning the command.

Glossary

ʿabd (pl. *ʿibād*): lit. slave; servant.
ʿAbdAllāh: Lit., "servant of God"
Abū Bakr aṣ-Ṣiddīq: the closest Companion of Prophet Muḥammad; the Prophet's father-in-law, who shared the *Hijrah* with him. After the Prophet's death, he was elected the first caliph (successor); known as one of the most saintly Companions.
Abū Yazīd/Bayāzīd Bistāmī: A great ninth century *walī* and a master of the Naqshbandi Golden Chain.
adab: good manners, proper etiquette.
adhān: call to prayer.
Ākhirah: the Hereafter; afterlife.
al-: Arabic definite article, "the".
ʿalāmīn: world; universes.
Alḥamdūlillāh: praise God.
ʿAlī ibn Abī Ṭālib: first cousin of Prophet Muḥammad, married to his daughter Fāṭimah; the fourth caliph.
alif: first letter of Arabic alphabet.
ʿAlīm, al-: the Knower, a divine attribute
Allāh: proper name for God in Arabic.
Allāhu Akbar: God is Greater.
ʿāmal: good deed (pl. *ʿamāl*).
amīr (pl., *umarā*): chief, leader, head of a nation or people.
anā: first person singular pronoun
anbīyā: prophets (sing. *nabī*).
ʿaql: intellect, reason; from the root *ʿaqila*: lit., "to fetter."
ʿArafah, ʿArafat: a plain near Mecca where pilgrims gather for the principal rite of Hajj.
ʿarif: knower, Gnostic; one who has reached spiritual knowledge of his Lord.
ʿĀrifūnʿ bil-Lāh: knowers of God.
Ar-Raḥīm: The Mercy-Giving, Merciful, Munificent, one of Allāh's ninety-nine Holy Names.
Ar-Raḥmān: The Most Merciful, Compassionate, Beneficent; the most repeated of Allāh's Holy Names.
ʿarsh, al-: the Divine Throne.
aṣl: root, origin, basis.
astāghfirullāh: lit. "I seek Allāh's forgiveness."
Awlīyāullāh: saints of Allāh (sing. *walī*).
āyah (pl. *ayāt*): a verse of the Holy Qur'an.
Āyat al-Kursī: "Verse of the Throne," a well-known supplication from the Qur'an (2:255).
ʿAzraʿīl: the Archangel of Death.
Badīʿ al-: The Innovator; a Divine Name.
Banī Ādam: Children of Adam; humanity.
Bayt al-Maqdis: the Sacred Mosque in Jerusalem, built at the site where Solomon's Temple was later erected.
Bayt al-Māʾmūr: much-frequented house; this refers to the Kaʿbah of the Heavens, which is the prototype of the Kaʿbah on Earth, circumambulated by the angels.
bayaʿ: pledge; in the context of this book, the pledge of initiation of a disciple (*murīd*) to a shaykh.
Bismillāhi'r-Raḥmāni'r-Raḥīm: "In the name of the All-Merciful, the All-Compassionate"; introductory verse to all chapters of the Qur'an, except the ninth.
Dajjāl: the False Messiah (Anti-Christ) will appear at the end-time of this

world, to deceive Mankind with false divinity.
dalālah: evidence.
dhāt: self / selfhood.
dhawq (pl. *adhwāq*): tasting; technical term referring to the experiential aspect of gnosis.
dhikr: remembrance, mention of God in His Holy Names or phrases of glorification.
dīyā: light.
Diwān al-Awlīyā: the nightly gathering of saints with Prophet Muḥammad in the spiritual realm.
du'ā: supplication.
dunyā: world; worldly life.
'Eid: festival; the two major celebrations of Islam are 'Eid al-Fitr, after Ramaḍān; and 'Eid al-Adha, the Festival of Sacrifice during the time of Hajj, which commemorates the sacrifice of Prophet Abraham.
fard: obligatory worship.
Fātiḥah: Sūratu 'l-Fātiḥah; the opening chapter of the Qur'an.
Ghafūr, al-: The Forgiver; one of the Holy Names of God.
Ghawth: lit. "Helper"; the highest rank of all saints.
ghaybu' l-muṭlaq, al-: the Absolute Unknown; known only to God.
ghusl: full shower/bath obligated by a state of ritual impurity, performed before worship.
Grandshaykh: generally, a *walī* of great stature. In this text, refers to Mawlana 'AbdAllāh ad-Daghestāni (d. 1973), Mawlana Shaykh Nazim's master.
hā': the Arabic letter ه
ḥadīth Nabawī (pl., *aḥadīth*): prophetic tradition whose meaning and linguistic expression are those of Prophet Muḥammad.
Ḥadīth Qudsī: divine saying whose meaning directly reflects the meaning God intended but whose linguistic expression is not divine speech as in the Qur'an.
ḥadr: present
Hajj: the sacred pilgrimage of Islam obligatory on every mature Muslim once in their life.
ḥalāl: permitted, lawful according to Islamic *Sharī'ah*.
Ḥaqīqah, al-: reality of existence; ultimate truth.
ḥaqq: truth
Ḥaqq, al-: the Divine Reality, one of the 99 Divine Names.
ḥarām: forbidden, unlawful.
ḥasanāt: good deeds.
hāshā: God forbid.
ḥarf: (pl. *ḥurūf*) letter; Arabic root "edge."
Ḥawā: Eve.
ḥaywān: animal.
Hijrah: emigration.
ḥikmah: wisdom.
ḥujjah: proof.
hūwa: the pronoun "he,"made up of the Arabic letters *hā'* and *wāw*.
'ibādu 'l-Lāh: servants of God.
'ifrīt: a type of *jinn*, huge and powerful.
iḥsān: doing good, "It is to worship God as though you see Him; for if you are not seeing Him, He sees you."
ikhlāṣ, al-: sincere devotion.
ilāh: (pl. *āliha*): idols or gods.
ilāhīyya: divinity.
ilhām: divine inspiration sent to *awlīyāullāh*.
'ilm: knowledge, science.
'Ilmu 'l-Awrāq: Knowledge of Papers.
'Ilmu 'l-Adhwāq: Knowledge of Taste.
'Ilmu 'l-Hurūf: Science of Letters.

ʿilmu ʾl-kalām: scholastic theology.
ʿilmun ladunnī: divinely inspired knowledge.
imān: faith, belief.
imām: leader of congregational prayer; an advanced scholar followed by a large community.
insān: humanity; pupil of the eye.
insānu ʾl-kāmil, al-: the Perfect Man, *i.e.*, Prophet Muḥammad.
irādatullāh: the Will of God.
irshād: spiritual guidance.
ism: name.
isma-Llāh: name of God.
isrāʿ: night journey; used here in reference to the night journey of Prophet Muḥammad.
Isrāʿfīl: Archangel Rafael, in charge of blowing the Final Trumpet.
jalāl: majesty.
jamāl: beauty.
jamaʿa: group, congregation.
Jannah: Paradise.
jihād: to struggle in God's Path.
Jibrīl: Gabriel, Archangel of revelation.
Jinn: a species of living beings created from fire, invisible to most humans. *Jinns* can be Muslim or non-Muslim.
Jumuʿah: Friday congregational prayer, held in a large mosque.
Kaʿbah: the first House of God, located in Mecca, Saudi Arabia to which pilgrimage is made and to which Muslims face in prayer.
kāfir: unbeliever.
Kalāmullāh al-Qadīm: lit., Allāh's Ancient Words, *viz.* the Holy Qur'an.
kalīmat at-tawḥīd: lā ilāha illa-Llāh: "There is no god but Al-Lāh (the God)."
karāmat: miracles.
khalīfah: deputy.
Khāliq, al-: the Creator, one of 99 Divine Names.
khalq: Creation.
khāniqah: designated smaller place for worship other than a mosque; *zāwiyah.*
khuluq: conduct, manners.
Kirāmun Kātabīn: honored Scribe angels.
lā: no; not; not existent; the particle of negation.
lā ilāha illa-Llāh Muḥammadun Rasūlullāh: There is no deity except Allāh, Muḥammad is the Messenger of Allāh.
lām: Arabic letter ل.
al-Lawḥ al-Maḥfūẓ: the Preserved Tablets.
Laylat al-Isrāʿ waʾl-Miʿrāj: the Night Journey and Ascension of Prophet Muḥammad to Jerusalem and to the Seven Heavens.
Madīnātu ʾl-Munawwara: the Illuminated city; city of Prophet Muḥammad; Madinah.
mahr: dowry, given by the groom to the bride.
Malakūt: Divine Kingdom.
Malik, al-: the Sovereign, a Divine Name.
Mālik: Archangel of Hell.
maqām: spiritual station; tomb of a prophet, messenger or saint.
maʿrifah: gnosis.
Māshāʾ Allāh: as Allāh Wills.
Mawlānā: lit. "Our master" or "our patron," referring to an esteemed person.
maẓhar: place of disclosure.
miḥrāb: prayer niche.
Mikāʿīl: Michael, Archangel of rain.
mīzān: the scale that weighs our deeds on Judgment Day.
mīm: Arabic letter م.

minbar: pulpit.
Miracles: of saints, known as *karamāt*; of prophets, known as *mu'jizāt* (lit., "That which renders powerless or helpless").
mi'rāj: the ascension of Prophet Muḥammad from Jerusalem to the Seven Heavens.
Muḥammadun rasūlu 'l-Lāh: Muḥammad is the Messenger of God.
mulk, al-: the World of dominion.
Mu'min, al-: Guardian of Faith, one of the 99 Names of God.
mu'min: a believer.
munājāt: invocation to God in a very intimate form.
Munkir: one of the angels of the grave.
murīd: disciple, student, follower.
murshid: spiritual guide; *pir*.
mushāhadah: direct witnessing.
mushrik (pl. *mushrikūn*): idolater; polytheist.
muwwāḥid (pl. *muwāḥḥidūn*): those who affirm God's Oneness.
nabī: a prophet of God.
nafs: lower self, ego.
Nakīr: the other angel of the grave (with Munkir).
nūr: light.
Nūḥ: the prophet Noah.
Nūr, an-: "The Source of Light"; a Divine Name.
Qādir, al-: "The Powerful"; a Divine Name.
qalam, al-: the Pen.
qiblah: direction, specifically, the direction faced by Muslims during prayer and other worship, towards the Sacred House in Mecca.
Quddūs, al-: "The Holy One"; a Divine Name.
qurb: nearness
quṭb (pl. *aqṭāb*): axis or pole. Among the poles are:
Quṭbu 'l-Bilād: Pole of the Lands.
Quṭbu 'l-Irshād: Pole of Guidance.
Quṭbu 'l-Aqṭāb: Pole of Poles.
Quṭbu 'l-A'dham: Highest Pole.
Quṭbu 'l-Mutaṣarrif: Pole of Affairs.
al-quṭbīyyatu 'l-kubrā: the highest station of poleship.
Rabb, ar-: the Lord.
Raḥīm, ar-: "The Most Compassionate"; a Divine Name.
Raḥmān, ar-: "The All-Merciful"; a Divine Name.
raḥmā: mercy.
raka'at: one full set of prescribed motions in prayer. Each prayer consists of a one or more *raka'ats.*
Ramaḍān: the ninth month of the Islamic calendar; month of fasting.
Rasūl: a messenger of God.
Rasūlullāh: the Messenger of God, Muḥammad ﷺ.
Ra'ūf, ar-: "The Most Kind"; a Divine Name.
Razzāq, ar-: "The Provider"; a Divine Name.
rawḥānīyyah: spirituality; spiritual essence of something.
Riḍwān: Archangel of Paradise.
rizq: provision; sustenance.
rūḥ: spirit. *Ar-Rūḥ* is the name of a great angel.
rukū': bowing posture of the prayer.
ṣadaqah: voluntary charity.
Ṣaḥābah (sing., *ṣaḥābī*): Companions of the Prophet; the first Muslims.
ṣaḥīḥ: authentic; term certifying validity of a *ḥadīth* of the Prophet.
ṣāim: fasting person (pl. *ṣāimūn*)
sajda (pl. *sujūd*): prostration.
ṣalāt: ritual prayer, one of the five obligatory pillars of Islam. Also, to invoke blessing on the Prophet.

Ṣalāt an-Najāt: prayer of salvation, offered in the late hours of night.
ṣalawāt (sing. *ṣalāt*): invoking blessings and peace upon the Prophet.
salām: peace.
Salām, as-: "The Peaceful"; a Divine Name. *As-salāmu ʿalaykum:* "Peace be upon you," the Islamic greeting.
Ṣamad, aṣ-: Self-Sufficient, upon whom creatures depend.
ṣawm, ṣiyām: fasting.
sayyi'āt: bad deeds; sins.
sayyid: leader; also, a descendant of Prophet Muḥammad.
Sayyīdinā: our master (fem. *sayyidunā; sayyidatunā*: our mistress).
shahādah: lit. testimony; the testimony of Islamic faith: *lā ilāha illa 'l-Lāh wa Muḥammadun rasūlu 'l-Lāh*, "There is no god but Allāh, the One God, and Muḥammad is the Messenger of God."
Shah Naqshband: Muḥammad Bahauddin Shah Naqshband, a great eighth century *walī,* and the founder of the Naqshbandi Ṭarīqah.
shaykh: lit. "old Man," a religious guide, teacher; master of spiritual discipline.
shifāʿ: cure.
shirk: polytheism, idolatry, ascribing partners to God
ṣiffāt: attributes; term referring to Divine Attributes.
Silsilat adh-dhahabīyya: "Golden Chain"of spiritual authority in Islam
sohbet (Arabic, *suḥbah*): association: the assembly or discourse of a shaykh.
subḥānAllāh: glory be to God.
sulṭān/sulṭānah: ruler, monarch.
Sulṭān al-Awlīyā: lit., "King of the *awlīyā*; the highest-ranking saint.
Sūnnah: Practices of Prophet Muḥammad in actions and words; what he did, said, recommended, or approved of in his Companions.
sūrah: a chapter of the Qur'an; picture, image.
Sūratu 'l-Ikhlāṣ: Chapter 114 of Holy Qur'an; the Chapter of Sincerity.
ṭabīb: doctor.
tābiʿīn: the Successors, one generation after the Prophet's Companions.
tafsīr: to explain, expound, explicate, or interpret; technical term for commentary or exegesis of the Holy Qur'an.
tajallī (pl. *tajallīyāt*): theophanies, God's self-disclosures, Divine Self-manifestation.
takbīr: lit. *"Allāhu Akbar,"*God is Great.
tarawīḥ: the special nightly prayers of Ramaḍān.
ṭarīqat/ṭarīqah: lit., way, road or path. An Islamic order or path of discipline and devotion under a guide or shaykh; Sufism.
taṣbīḥ: recitation glorifying or praising God.
tawāḍaʿ: humbleness.
ṭawāf: the rite of circumambulating the Kaʿbah while glorifying God during Hajj and ʿUmra.
tawḥīd: unity; universal or primordial Islam, submission to God, as the sole Master of destiny and ultimate Reality.
Tawrāt: Torah
tayammum: Alternate ritual ablution performed in the absence of water.
ʿubūdīyyah: state of worshipfulness; servanthood.
ʿulamā (sing. *ʿālim*): scholars.
ʿulūmu 'l-awwalīna wa 'l-ākhirīn: Knowledge of the "Firsts"and the

"Lasts" refers to the knowledge God poured into the heart of Prophet Muḥammad during his Holy Ascension to the Divine Presence.
'ulūm al-Islāmī: Islamic religious sciences.
Ummāh: faith community, nation.
'Umar ibn al-Khaṭṭāb: an eminent Companion of Prophet Muḥammad and second caliph of Islam.
'umra: the minor pilgrimage to Mecca, performed at any time of the year.
'Uthmān ibn 'Affān: eminent Companion of the Prophet; his son-in-law and third caliph of Islam, renowned for compiling the Qur'an.
walad: a child.
waladī: my child.
walāyah: proximity or closeness; sainthood.
walī (pl. *awlīyā*): saint, or "he who assists"; guardian; protector.
wasīlah: a means; holy station of Prophet Muḥammad as God's intermediary to grant supplications.
wāw: Arabic letter و
wujūd, al-: existence; "to find," "the act of finding," and "being found."
Y'aqūb: Jacob; the prophet.
yamīn: the right hand; previously meant "oath."
Yawm al-'ahdi wa'l-mīthāq: Day of Oath and Covenant, a heavenly event before this Life, when all souls of humanity were present to God, and He took from each the promise to accept His Sovereignty as Lord.
yawm al-qiyāmah: Day of Judgment.
Yūsuf: Joseph; the prophet.
zāwiyah: designated smaller place for worship other than a mosque; also *khāniqah*.
zīyāra: visitation to the grave of a prophet, a prophet's companion or a saint.

Other Publications

Maulana Shaykh Nazim Adil al-Haqqani

- Heavenly Showers (2012)
- The Sufilive Series (2010-2011)
- Breaths from Beyond the Curtain (2010)
- In the Eye of the Needle
- The Healing Power of Sufi Meditation
- The Path to Spiritual Excellence
- In the Mystic Footsteps of Saints (2 volumes)
- Liberating the Soul (6 volumes)

Shaykh Hisham Kabbani

- The Prohibition of Domestic Violence in Islam (2011)
- The Sufilive Series (2010-2011)
- Cyprus Summer Series (2 volumes)
- The Ninefold Ascent
- Who Are the Guides?
- Illuminations
- Banquet for the Soul
- Symphony of Remembrance
- The Healing Power of Sufi Meditation
- In the Shadow of Saints
- Keys to the Divine Kingdom
- The Sufi Science of Self-Realization
- Universe Rising: the Approach of Armageddon?
- Pearls and Coral (2 volumes)
- Classical Islam and the Naqshbandi Sufi Tradition
- The Naqshbandi Sufi Way
- Encyclopedia of Islamic Doctrine (7 volumes)
- Angels Unveiled
- Encyclopedia of Muḥammad's Women Companions and the Traditions They Related

Hajjah Amina Adil

- Muḥammad: the Messenger of Islam
- The Light of Muḥammad
- Lore of Light / Links of Light
- My Little Lore of Light (3 volumes)

Hajjah Naziha Adil Kabbani

- Secrets of Heavenly Food (2009)
- Heavenly Foods (2011)

CPSIA information can be obtained
at www.ICGtesting.com
Printed in the USA
FFOW051141200313
1014FF

9 781938 058035